A N
UNSU
GAME

Celebrating
Scottish Women's Football
Fifty Years After the Ban

Karen Fraser
Julie McNeill
Fiona Skillen
(Editors)

TIPPERMUIR
· BOOKS LIMITED ·

This first edition published and copyright 2024 by
Tippermuir Books Ltd, Perth, Scotland.
mail@tippermuirbooks.co.uk – www.tippermuirbooks.co.uk.

ISBN 978-1-913836-41-2 (paperback).

A CIP catalogue record for this book is available from the British Library.

Project coordination and editorial by Paul S Philippou.
Cover image by Katie Kelman (City of Glasgow College).
Cover design by Matthew Mackie.
Editorial support: Ajay Close and Steve Zajda.
Co-founders and publishers of Tippermuir Books:
Rob Hands, Matthew Mackie and Paul S Philippou.
Text design, layout and artwork by Bernard Chandler [graffik].
Text set in Janson Text LT Std 10.5/13pt with Metropolis titling.

Printed and bound by Ashford Colour Press.

This book has been printed in the UK to reduce transportation miles and their
impact upon the environment. It has been printed to comply with the Forest
Stewardship Council (FSC) Chain of Custody requirements and paper
sourcing from responsibly managed sources.

'*Tenacity, prowess and passion. This book is a celebration of women's resilience and strength – it tells the untold tales of women's football through poems, stories and reminiscences. Fiona, Karen and Julie have created a long overdue celebration of the determination and passion that became the foundation of the modern game.*'
Eddi Reader

'*A celebration of resilience. This is our game, this is our ball, this is our history, this is our future.*'
Rose Reilly

'*A wonderful celebration of the pioneering women footballers who campaigned so hard to take their rightful place in the beautiful game.*'
Kirsty Wark

*To all the women and girls who laid the ground, thank you for your strength and persistence in the face of great adversity and for our own trailblazers: Lewis [**Fiona**], Kellen and Maya [**Karen**] and Shea and Bella [**Julie**].*

They show her
what women

can do when
we raise each other.
She believes in

the women who
save themselves,
the girls standing

ready to gie it laldy
shoulder to shoulder
before her.

ACKNOWLEDGEMENTS

THE EDITORS wish to acknowledge the many people, who in different ways have contributed to this book. The origins of this collection are firmly rooted in The Hampden Collection, which was set up in 2017 to preserve and promote Scotland's pioneering footballing history through the magnificent story of the three Hampden Parks and all who played on them. The Hampden Collection is made up of talented, dedicated volunteers (including poets, artists, historians, tour guides, bowlers, cricketers and football fans) who are committed to bringing the stories and legacy of The Hampden Parks to a wider audience. The editors met through their involvement in The Hampden Collection.

Many of the poems were written and originally in The Hampden Collection's 'World Home of Football Poetry' website. The Hampden Collection created its poetry section on 26 March 2018, with Stephen Watt as its inaugural Poet-in-Chief. Stephen handed over the baton to Jim Mackintosh in 2019, with Julie McNeill taking over, as current poetry leader in late 2021, where she was joined by a team of fitba Makars – Stuart Kenny, Susi Briggs, Gabrielle Barnby and Hugh McMillan – heading up collections celebrating the men, women and children of the game. Submissions to the poetry section came from poets from all over the world, united in their passion for the beautiful game. We have been lucky enough to select a range of poems from this rich body of work to add to this book as well as commissioning new work from some of the brightest and best poets in Scotland. We are grateful to The Hampden Collection and the poets who have trusted us with their work and for their enthusiasm and support for this project. We would especially like to thank Graeme Brown, Barry Kirk, Richard S Young, Lindsay Hamilton, David Coutts and Ashley Rawson.

This project joins a series of other projects Karen and Fiona have been working on around uncovering the history of the women's game in Scotland. They, along with Andy Mitchell, have been working closely with the Scottish Football Association to trace international players from 1972 until 1997 in order that they can be finally awarded caps for representing Scotland.

We would like to use this opportunity to encourage anyone who has any information about former international players to please contact us directly.

The editors would also like to thank Paul S Philippou from Tippermuir Books for supporting this project right from the very start when it was little more than a few ideas and a burning passion to share the stories of the women's game. Thank you Paul for having faith in our ideas and giving us a platform to share them. Thanks go also to members of the Tippermuir Team: Bernard Chandler (graphics), Matthew Mackie (cover designer) and Steve Zajda (proof-reader).

Our heartfelt thanks to Ashley Rawson and his HND students at City of Glasgow College who undertook a project to design the cover for this book. We are grateful to all of them for their care and talent, the decision was not an easy one! The chosen cover was designed by HND student Katie Kelman who understood the brief brilliantly and brought a freshness to the subject matter. Thank you to Ashley, Katie and City of Glasgow College for their input and enthusiasm. We have loved working with you.

Finally, everyone who has contributed to this book has given their time and labour for free. Royalties from this book will be donated to a Women's Recreational Football project to help support the game at a grassroots level. We hope this will encourage more women and girls to keep playing the game they love.

Acknowledgement and gratitude is offered for permission to include the following poems, song lyrics and prose.

Gabrielle Barnby, 'Grief', published online at The Hampden Collection (March 2023).

Paul Beeson and **Bruce Strachan**, 'Lace Up Our Boots' and 'Winning Working Women', *Sweet F.A.* (Tippermuir Books, 2022).

Graeme Brown, 'Bravehearts', published online at The Hampden Collection (June 2020).

Laura Carberry, 'This Poem is For Ma Daughter', published online at The Hampden Collection (February 2023).

Thomas Clark, 'By Ony Ither Name', published online at The Hampden Collection (August 2022).

Peter Clive, 'A Curler to Remember', published online at The Hampden Collection (August 2022).

Maya Halcrow, 'Matchday', published online at The Hampden Collection (July 2022).

Jackie Kay, 'Girl Footballer', *The Frog Who Thought She Was an Opera Singer* (Bloomsbury 1998).

Jim Mackintosh, 'Erin', published online at The Hampden Collection (January 2020) and 'The Steel Veined Pioneers, *Nutmeg* football magazine (October 2023).

Rose Macgregor, 'In Mither's Fit Steps', published online at The Hampden Collection (June 2022).

Julie McNeill, 'The Women Before Her', 'History' and 'Phenomenal', *We are Scottish Football* (Luath, 2024).

David McVey, 'Tynecastle October 2020', published online at The Hampden Collection (July 2020).

Abiy Orr, The Crowd's Love Song', published online at The Hampden Collection (May 2021).

Jane Patience, 'Goalie Gloves', published online at The Hampden Collection (September 2022).

Gayle Smith, 'Hold the Front Page', published online at The Hampden Collection (August 2021).

Gerda Stevenson, 'Scotland celebrates 3–0 at Easter Road', *Quines: Poems in Tribute to Women of Scotland* (Luath Press, 2020).

WOMEN'S RECREATIONAL FOOTBALL

All the royalties from this book will be donated to the advancement of Women's Recreational Football:

'Women's recreational football is a place for women to play the game regardless of age, ability and experience. It's a place for women to support women to play the beautiful game.'

Sam Milne,
Club Development Officer, Scottish FA

Contents

FOR THE LOVE OF THE GAME *p.55*

PIONEERS & HEROINES *p*.101

SCOTLAND *p.*149

BAIRNS & LASSIES *p.*213

FOREWORD

WE COULD THINK of none better to write the foreword to this book than three women who are involved in women's football at the most senior level in the Scottish game. We were delighted when all three agreed.

'It still amazes me when I'm at events or discussing the history of women's football, just how many people are completely unaware of the 50-year ban and the huge battle that women and girls have faced.

A battle just to be able to play the beautiful game. As proud Chair of Scottish Women's Football, we have pushed to raise the profile of our game not only to encourage more women and girls to participate, but to show organisations that our game in worth investing in.

The tireless work that our invaluable historians do is absolutely essential not only in shining a light on the inspiring stories of women who faced similar battles to what we are still facing today, but in also raising awareness that these challenges have not disappeared.

Women and girls must be given equal opportunities in football. This piece of work is one of a kind and I cannot wait to read it.'

Viv MacLaren
Chair, Scottish Women's Football

'Books that focus on the history of women's football and celebrate its participants play a vital role in promoting gender equality, inspiring young athletes, preserving historical narratives and providing much-needed recognition to female athletes who have made a significant contribution to our game in Scotland. It is imperative that the achievements of women in football are not lost to future generations.'

Shirley Martin
Head of Girls' and Women's Football,
Scottish Football Association

'As Managing Director of the Scottish Women's Premier League I find it incredible to see the development of the game in recent years, with more professional players than ever playing in the League. The opportunity for women to make a living out of football is so important if we are to advance and inspire the next generation to continue to pursue that progress. This was unimaginable 50 years ago when the restrictions on women's football were lifted. This book celebrates the women who fought to play the game from the Victorian era onwards; these women laid the foundations that we continue to build on today. The stories shared in this collection highlight the rich history of the women's game that every fan should know and we should all be proud of.'

Fiona McIntyre
Managing Director,
Scottish Women's Premier League

INTRODUCTION
Karen Fraser, Julie McNeill & Fiona Skillen

THIS COLLECTION has been drawn together to celebrate the long and important history of women's football in Scotland. Often perceived as a relatively new sport for women, taken up in the wake of second-wave feminism, or ladette culture, the overlooked reality is that women have been playing football in Scotland continuously for over a century and its roots can be traced back hundreds of years. Women have had to fight for opportunities to play the game they love. They have been banned and discriminated against. They have faced hostility and sexism. And yet, they persevered and found ways to play.

Because playing football as a women or girl has, until recently, been viewed as something controversial and involving small numbers of women, this rich history has been overlooked, ignored or 'hidden'. Our collection is therefore about shining a light onto the stories and experiences of the women and girls who have played the beautiful game in Scotland at all levels and in all settings. We want to reflect the stories of those who played for formal teams, those who represented Scotland, and those who played informally in their local streets, backcourts or parks. What comes across from these stories and poems is a passion for playing football, the joy that the game provides regardless of where it is played and the sense of community and connection that it creates amongst those who play it or support a team.

This is not a traditional poetry book. We have tried to bring together poems, essays, interviews, history and the experiences of the women who played in order to give you a deeper understanding of the development of the game and to celebrate those who have driven the game forward. We have included the words of the players, coaches and administrators themselves, as who better to tell it like it was? We have included short essays

1

on the history and development of the game and the poetry you will read here has been inspired by all of these stories. The book is divided into sections around loose themes. In doing so we hope that you can enjoy reading it cover-to-cover or dip in and out of each section.

The history of the women's game is evolving all the time. Developments in the current women's game are happening quickly. It is an exciting time to be involved in women's football, as a player, organiser or fan. The increasing global and local interest in the women's game, spurred on by the two most recent Olympics, Women's Euros and Women's World Cup, has seen the number of women and girls playing in Scotland grow. Significantly, as reported by the SFA on 18 January 2024 (scottishfa.co.uk), in 2023, 22,977 women and girls were registered with the SFA as grassroots players. This growth, coupled with the development of professional football for women has meant that the game is being given more media coverage and investment than ever before. There is still some way to go in terms of equality of investment, sponsorship and media coverage but the signs of positive growth are there to be seen. It is therefore important at this juncture that we pause to reflect on how far the game has come and to pay our respects and thanks to those who pioneered it. Their history has been hidden away and overlooked for too long, and yet without these pioneers both on the pitch and off it, the gains of today would have been even harder to achieve.

This collection is an opportunity to set out that long history for the first time and to give voice to the women who made that history. It is a celebration of the achievements of them, those who came after and the women and girls playing today, through words and poetry.

HISTORY

Julie McNeill

The Scotland first eleven shine
from a poster on her bedroom wall:
Caroline, Martha, Jamie-Lee.

I try to trace the thread
following the line that brought
us to this settled ground

piecing together scrolling, scrolling
I find snippets in footnotes,
addendums, clues buried

in unrelated places
obscure articles and
off-the-cuff comments.

Headlines such as: 'Are you near

Fir Park tomorrow? Take the wife
with you to see the lady footballers.'

Threads fray and fuse

before I find the end.
It's like holding mist

in your fingertips
wondering where

did your history go?

WOMEN'S FOOTBALL IN SCOTLAND:
A TIMELINE
Fiona Skillen & Karen Fraser

1628
Earliest existing records of women's football.

1795
Reverend Dr Alexander Carlisle, *Statistical Account for the Parish of Inveresk* (1795), records the annual fishwives' football match.

7 May 1881
First women's international, Scotland vs England, is played at Hibernian Park, Edinburgh, 3–0.

16 May 1881
Second women's international match, Shawfield, Glasgow. Match abandoned due to crowd pitch invasion.

1 May 1895
British Ladies' Football Club tour Scotland. Match played at St Mirren's grounds in Paisley on 1 May 1895 in front of 6,000 spectators. Positive public support was sorely lacking, and matches were once again blighted by rioting protestors, indeed that first game in Paisley ended with the players being escorted by the police to the pavilion after the crowd broke onto the pitch.

1914–18
The First World War sees women's teams flourish across Scotland for the duration of the war. Over 60 matches are played between 1917 and 1918.

1921
Founding of Rutherglen Ladies FC – the premier women's team of interwar Scotland.

December 1921
The FA introduce a 'ban' on women's football in England. Scotland do not formally ban women's football but to all intents and purposes most SFA-affiliated clubs refuse to host women's games.

September 1949
The SFA formally minute a 'ban' on women playing on affiliated pitches, although an informal ban had been in place for decades.

1950s and 1960s
Women continue to play football throughout this period although records are limited. Across the 1960s, there is a steady growth of teams with a minimum of 60 teams playing across the decade.

1970/71
Connectiveness among teams in Scotland begins to grow. Links with the English Women's Football Association (WFA) which had been formed in 1969 are strengthened and Scottish club teams do well in several competitions based in England including the Deal International Tournament and the Butlin's Cup.

18 April 1971
Inaugural final of the Women's Scottish Cup between Stewarton Thistle and Aberdeen Prima Donnas. This started as an invitation tournament but quickly became an open competition.

8 May 1971
Stewarton Thistle reach the final of the first Mitre Cup competition run by the English Women's Football Association.

June 1971
UEFA Members vote 31–1 in favour of recognising the women's game within their countries. Scotland is the only country which votes against the motion.

17 September 1972

The Scottish Women's Football Association (SWFA) is established with six teams. It affiliates to the WFA but is not recognised by the SFA.

September 1972

The first official women's league is formed. By the end of the year, it has twelve participating teams.

18 November 1972

First women's international, Scotland vs England, is played at Ravenscraig Park, Greenock. 0–3.

29 August 1974

The SFA recognise women's football, effectively lifting the 'ban', but do not affiliate the SWFA.

Late 1970s

A great deal of football is being played, some within the 'official' organisation of the SWFA but there are also many more teams playing who have chosen not to join the SWFA.

September 1982

The Scottish Women's National Team (SWNT) plays its first match in an official UEFA Women's Championship.

Across the 1980s

There continues to be a great deal of women's football played. There are a small number of official leagues but these are supplemented by competitions run by the SWFA and other community organisations. In the mid-1980s, in addition to league games, teams could be involved in a pre-season tournament in Dundee, a league cup for their division, the Scottish Cup, a mid-season tournament in Paisley, the end of season Leven Cup and two national 5-a-side tournaments. Alongside these, there were many informal competitions. The SWFA works hard to develop and promote women's football.

1992

Shelia Begbie is appointed to role of Girls' and Women's Football Co-ordinator as part of the Scottish Sports Council's Team Sport Scotland initiative. She works with the SWFA and SFA to develop women's football. By 1993, funding has been secured for a full-time administration post to support the SWFA and they are provided with an office at SFA headquarters. The same year, after a protracted campaign, women can commence the coaching qualification pathway.

1995

Shelia Begbie and Maggi Wilson become the first women in Scotland to pass the UEFA A Licence.

Late 1997

It was agreed that the SFA would take over management of the SWNT and strategic development of the women's and girls' game.

February 1998

The SWFA granted affiliation to the SFA.

Summer 1998

The SFA appoint Vera Pauw to the National Lottery funded post of national coach and technical director, the first time the position has been a paid one.

1999

The Scottish Women's Football League (SWFL) is set up as separate organisation, though still part of SWFA with the intention of improving standards, building communications, attracting sponsorship, improving administration and 'professionalisation'.

June 2000

The SWFA formally agrees to become a limited company.

2001

The SWFA becomes Scottish Women's Football (SWF).

2002

The Scottish Women's Premier League (SWPL) is formed – still as part of the SWFA and with the SWFL continuing.

2005

Anna Signeul is appointed as the new SWNT manager. Her predecessor, Pauw, had worked to improve the team and now Signeul looks to take this to the next stage by supporting clubs to build a platform for the growth and development of women's football in Scotland which would be of benefit to all. She and Begbie work with the SWF and the SFA to deliver workshops, training, and a tour of Swedish clubs.

2012

The first time the SWNT plays at Hampden.

2017

The SWNT take part in their first UEFA Women's championship finals in the Netherlands.

2018

As a result of a sponsorship deal, for the first time, prize money can be awarded to the winners of the women's leagues.

2019

As part of a project to recognise those women who played for the SWNT prior to the SFA management, the first players from the 1972 match are capped by the SFA at Hampden.

2019

The SWNT take part in their first World Cup tournament at the FIFA Women's World Cup France 2019™.

Mid 2021

The SFA completes its review of elite women's football and begins discussions about the proposed recommendations.

July 2021

The SFA announces that home games for international tournaments are to be played at Hampden.

March 2022

Following negotiations with the SWF and a vote by clubs, the women's SPFL is formed under a separate board. Seventeen clubs leave the SWF and move to the SPFL.

July 2022

Fiona McIntyre is appointed as Managing Director of the Women's SPFL.

October 2022

The remaining players from the 1972 Ravenscraig Pioneers team are capped at Hampden. The project to recognise all the women who played for the SWNT while it was under the management of the SWFA continues.

April 2024

Having failed to qualify for the UEFA Women's Championship in 2022 and the Women's World Cup in 2023, the SWNT are seeking qualification for the UEFA Women's Championship in 2025.

Origins & Early Years

In this section you will find poems and short essays about the very early history of women's football from the Musselburgh fishwives through to the factory teams of the First World War and the introduction of the 'Ban'.

The women's game in Scotland has a long, long history of which we should be proud. For centuries, women who wanted to play football have faced and overcome adversity in order to play a sport they loved.

THE ORIGINS OF
WOMEN'S FOOTBALL IN SCOTLAND
Fiona Skillen

WOMEN'S FOOTBALL in Scotland has a long history. The earliest record of women's football dates from 1628 when a Minister recorded his frustration at his parishioners breaking the Sabbath 'by the insolent behaviour of men and women in footballing, dancing and Barley Breaks'.

Women playing football is mentioned again in, as we can see here, in 1795, when Reverend Dr Alexander Carlisle, notes in that year's *Statistical Account for the Parish of Inveresk*:

> As [the fishwives] do the work of men, their manners are masculine and their strength and activity is equal to their work...their amusements are more of the masculine kind. On holidays they frequently play golf and on Shrove Tuesday there is a standing match at football between the married and unmarried women, at which the former are always victors.

It has been suggested that the fact that the married women always won meant the game was more of a ritual than a competition.

However, it is in the late Victorian period that we really see the modern game of women's football emerging. Taking place just seven years after the first men's football international (also between Scotland and England), and in a period when the then relatively-young Football Association was still locked in bitter wars with its rivals to establish a common set of basic rules for the game, this 'rather novel' women's game provided a fascinating perspective on the place of women's football in late nineteenth-century Britain.

On 7 May 1881 at 3pm, the first ever 'international' match in the UK was played at Hibernian Park, Easter Road in Edinburgh.

The teams were promoted as Scotland versus England, but the recruitment and selection process is unclear. What seems evident is that the players were actresses or dancers drawn from the theatre and music hall scene by the theatrical agents who staged these early games. The teams were comprised of the following players (based on various newspaper reports of the match):

Scotland

Ethel Hay, Bella Osborne, Georgina Wright, Rose Raynham, Isa Stevenson, Louise Cole, Carrie Baliol, Emma Wright, Lily St Clair, Maud Riverford and Minnie Brymner.

England

May Godwin, Mabel Bradbury, Maude Hopewell, Maude Starling, Ada Everston, Mabel Vance, Kate Mellor, Geraldine Ventnor, Eva Davenport, Minnie Hopewell and Nellie Sherwood.

The match was widely reported in Scotland and further afield and from news articles we can piece together a lot of information about the match. The match was attended by between 1,000 and 2,000 mainly male spectators. It ended 3–0 in favour of Scotland, with the first goal scored by Lily St Clair. *The Dunfermline Journal* reporting on the match noted that almost half of the crowd left before the end of the match. *The Glasgow Herald* of 9 May 1881 reported:

> A rather novel football match took place at Easter Road, Edinburgh on Saturday between teams of lady players representing England and Scotland – the former hailing from London and the latter, it is said from Glasgow. A considerable amount of curiosity was evinced in the event, and upwards of a thousand persons witnessed it. The young ladies' ages appeared

to range from eighteen to four-and twenty, and they were very smartly dressed.

Adverts and reports of the match in the press show that this inaugural 'Ladies' international was dismissed as little more than a curio – an entertainment somewhere between a fashion parade and a contemporary (if mild) Victorian freak show. They noted that most spectators took the match less than seriously and 'were pretty free with their criticisms, not only of the play, but of the appearance and behaviour of the players, treating the various episodes and accidents of the game with sarcastic or personal remarks, and with loud guffaws'. Overall, the 'general feeling seemed to be that the whole affair was an unfeminine exhibition'.

A week after their debut in Edinburgh, the teams took to the field in Glasgow for a 'return' match and, in the span of just seven days, public opinion appeared to have turned against the women footballers. On the morning of Friday, 20 May 1881, provincial newspapers across Britain carried reports of the match.

Under the headline, 'Ladies' 'International' Football Match' the *Nottinghamshire Guardian* informed its readers:

> What will probably be the first and last exhibition of a female football match in Glasgow took place on Monday evening at Shawfield Grounds...The meagre training of the teams did not augur much for proficiency of play, and if the display of football tactics was of a sorry description, it was only what might have been expected, and not much worse than some of the efforts of our noted football clubs.

The crowd initially subjected the players to faintly bawdy banter. Then, in an unsettling precursor of modern soccer hooliganism, in the 55th minute of the match ribaldry turned to violence:

At last a few roughs broke into the enclosure, and as these were followed by hundreds soon after, the players were roughly jostled, and had prematurely to take refuge in the omnibus which had conveyed them to the ground. Their troubles were not, however, yet ended, for the crowd tore up the stakes and threw them at the departing vehicle, and but for the presence of the police, some bodily injury to the females might have occurred...The team of four grey horses [pulling the omnibus] was driven rapidly from the ground amid the jeers of the crowd, and the players escaped with, let us hope, nothing worse than a serious fright.

With a third match between the 'Scottish' and 'English' teams then cancelled, Helen Matthews decided to try her luck on the other side of the border, organising a series of games in Blackburn, Liverpool and Manchester. She quickly encountered familiar opposition.

So, in a matter of just a few of weeks the modern game of women's football in Scotland had been born and crushed by public opinion. There were few further attempts to stage women's games and the sport essentially disappeared for another fourteen years. When the game did re-emerge in 1895, in the form of the British Ladies' Football Club, it once again quickly foundered on the rocks of prejudice and misogyny. The team's first match in Scotland was played at St Mirren's grounds in Paisley on 1 May 1895 in front of 6,000 spectators. The ladies 'were attired in blue knickerbockers, some also having skirts to their knees'. 'The play from commencement to finish was the occasion of continuous and hearty laughter.' The match was described by a journalist in the *Paisley & Renfrewshire Gazette* as 'the most ridiculous exhibition I have ever seen in my life'.

Despite clear public interest or at least curiosity, crowds of several thousand watched many of the games, positive public support was sorely lacking, and matches were once again blighted by rioting protestors. Indeed, that first game in Paisley ended with the players being escorted by the police to the pavilion after the crowd broke onto the pitch. Before long, this second attempt to establish women's football was abandoned until the outbreak of the Great War.

PELTED

Julie McNeill

The story is potted
and familiar
the duck-and-weave
we associate with
the flight-of-foot:

lightweight boxers,
small prey animals,
the Highlanders
strike and hide.
When faced

with a dominant
force is there
any other way?
At first they were
a freak show:

a display of vulgarity
and curiosity. Whack!
Then a fashion parade:
the shoes,
blue knickerbockers

knee-length skirts.
Whack! Next an
exhibition – let the ladies
entertain. Greet

them with your
loud guffaws.
Whack!
Whack!
Whack!

Before long curled fists
ripped up
stakes, ran them off
the grass,
pelted in shame.

Four grey horses
bid them escape.
Heads did go down.
Then up they popped
again

to be greeted with
a firm and final Whack!
Laughter from the start
until this ridiculous exhibition
is over. Slapped down

again in this game of
whack-a-mole
they stay down this time,
out of the light
out of sight.

When gunfire
gave cover
women emerged.
Some with balls
at their feet

many using their
own names,
factories fizzing
with them.
They will be whacked

down again, of course
and again, and again
they'll play
the long game
gain ground

in inches and know
that every
blade of grass
is land
hard won.

SCOTLAND CELEBRATES 3–0
AT EASTER ROAD
Gerda Stevenson

ETHEL HAY (goal), Bella Osbourne and Georgina Wright (backs), Rose Rayman and Isa Stevenson (half-backs), Emma Wright, Louise Cole, Lily St Clair, Maud Riweford, Carrie Balliol and Minnie Brymner (forwards) wearing knickerbockers in the style of the Rational Dress movement, played and won the first recorded women's international football match, Scotland vs England, Saturday, 7 May 1881, Easter Road, Edinburgh.

The wind was against us – but wasn't it ever?
We had all to play for, and nothing to lose;
we kicked off with gusto, no matter the weather,
two thousand, the crowd, their jeers couldn't bruise
our spirits; red stockings and belts a kindling flicker
across the turf, then flashes of fire, flames fanned
by self-belief, we were bonded as one, slicker
than our English sisters, that day; we spanned
the field, every inch covered, Ethel hardly required
in goal – but when her moment came, oh, the spring
in her fearless lunge to save – the whole team fired!
We surge forward, and hear someone sing,
a lone voice at first, *Daughters of Freedom Arise*,
then more and more: *Yield not the battle till ye have won!* –
our striker takes possession, her mind on the prize,
Lily St Clair, talk about flair! – a meteor cast from the sun –
Dancing and dodging, she blazes to the box, and bends
the ball in – a goal for Scotland! We weep and cheer,
Scotia's Eleven makes history, sends
a message to the world: have no doubt, we are here,
scaling the heights, new horizons in our sights
and the ball is rolling for women's rights.

EARLY WOMEN'S FOOTBALL AND THE SPORTS ENTREPRENEUR

Stuart Gibbs

THE INVOLVEMENT of women in early folk football is now well–established. At Carstairs in 1628, the first reference to women playing the game in Europe, the village matches between Coldstream and Lennel of 1786 and the ad hoc matches played by disadvantaged girls of parish and industrial schools during the 1860s and early 1870s have been well documented.[1] However, it is only recently that the historiography of women's football as an organised sport has been tackled in earnest, and the initial findings show a strong link to the entertainment industry. The success of Scotland vs England internationals encouraged the theatre entrepreneurs Alec Gordon and George Frederick Charles to organise their novelty Scotland vs England matches featuring women's teams.

George Frederick Charles was born George Imbert in London in 1822.[2] He was successful as an actor and theatre manager in London and the north of England but by the late 1870s, Frederick Charles was operating an advertising agency out of St Helens. Alec Gordon was reportedly born in Edinburgh and ran a theatrical business in the north of England in partnership with the actor W H Pitt.[3] The Pitt and Gordon Company enjoyed modest success but when Pitt died in 1879 Gordon's fortunes began to falter. The financial positions of both Charles and Gordon were disadvantaged so the football tour was developed not so much to garner profit but to generate capital in a bid to rejuvenate their flagging careers.

At least 2,000 spectators were attracted to Charles and Gordon's first Scotland vs England game at Hibernian's old Easter Road ground on 7 May 1881. Goals from Lily St Clair and Louise Cole helped secure a 3–0 win for the Scotland side.[4] Crowd disturbances at a second match at Shawfield Running

Track in Rutherglen resulted in a court order preventing further fixtures forcing the teams to move south. Matches at Blackburn Olympics ground, Sheffield and Halifax attracted healthy crowds but further disturbances at Cheetham FC's ground in Manchester led to one match being cancelled.[5] The sides had better luck in Liverpool where the tour was wound up after three matches played between 25 and 28 June 1881.[6] With the proceeds, Gordon moved to Dublin where he was the leaseholder of the Queen's Theatre whereas Frederick Charles refurbished the St Helens Theatre Royal, which he ran until his retirement in 1884.

Following the 1881 tour, other entrepreneurs staged women's football matches attracted by their earning potential. George Soule of the Hull Alhambra Palace developed an act – the Football Ballet – in which girls' teams played mock matches on stage to appreciative audiences across the country. Open-air matches were also staged but these were not greeted so enthusiastically, with pitch invasions taking place in Hull and at the second Hampden Park in 1884 and at the East End Ground, Hull, in 1887.[7]

The most famous of the early women's sides was the British Ladies' Football Club. Founded by the Smith family in the autumn of 1894, Alfred Hewitt Smith was the club's manager while his younger sister, Phoebe, sister-in-law, Jessie Allen, and wife, Hannah Oliphant, all took the role of either club captain or secretary. Hewitt Smith, an estate agent to trade, had the ambition to work in entertainment and he formed the British Ladies' Football Club as a means of establishing a new career as a promoter. Alongside football matches, Hewitt Smith often staged after-match shows featuring local variety acts but also the players themselves. Phoebe Smith for instance often ventured on stage at these events. Ellen Dunn who played for the club as Ruth Coupland, was also on stage at Hewitt Smith's post-match soirées; she appeared under the name Lily Flexmore.[8]

Dunn used her association with the British Ladies' Club as her stage apprenticeship. When she left the club in 1897, her early professional stage appearances as Lily Flexmore were at the Empire Theatre in Johannesburg, and, by 1908, she was performing in the US in vaudeville and the Orpheum Circuit.[9]

Another prominent player with the British Ladies' was Helen Matthew who appeared as Mrs Graham or Helen Graham Matthews. Matthew claimed she was born in Montrose but she hailed from Exmouth in Devon and only had family connections to the northeast of Scotland. Brought up in Liverpool during the 1880s, Matthew began playing football with her sister, Florence, in 'Ladies vs Gentlemen' matches organised by the showman Alec Payne.[10] The Matthew sisters also edited a sports column titled the 'Lothian Lasses' which appeared in the *Football & Cricket Field*, *Liverpool Echo* and the *Lancashire Evening News*, which covered the Lancashire football scene and in particular their favourite side, Preston North End. Besides being football pioneers, the sisters can be counted among the lists of female sports entrepreneurs.[11]

Helen Matthew appeared in goal for the British Ladies' Football Club's debut at Crouch End, London, on 23 March 1895 and was an ever-present during the club's subsequent tours during 1895. Later that year, she headed up a second-string tour consisting of Mrs Graham's XI, and resident opposition, London & District. And when Florence Matthew returned to football during the early months of 1896, Mrs Graham's XI adopted the sisters' old column name 'Lothian Lasses' for matches in Preston, Darwin and Southport, which were refereed by sports all-rounder Frank Sugg.[12]

Mrs Graham's XI eventually collapsed after a three-month tour of Scotland in July 1896.[13] The main British Ladies' Football Club continued until 1907 after which Alfred Hewitt Smith moved on to be involved in the roller-skating craze of the 1900s.[14] It is commonly thought that football went into a hiatus after the British Ladies' folded to be revived during the Great War; however, women's matches continued to be played, such as that at Cathkin Park in 1914 between the cast of the pantomime 'Tommy Ticker' and the theatrical matches played at White Hart Lane between 1912 and 1914.[15] Women's football continued to have a strong connection to entertainment well into the twentieth century.

'THE MUNITION AND FACTORY GIRLS HAVE CAUGHT FOOTBALL FEVER': WOMEN'S FOOTBALL IN SCOTLAND 1914–1918
Fiona Skillen

THE OUTBREAK OF the First World War was an important point in the development of women's football. There was, a critical shift in the types of occupations women had in this period. Before the war, women had mostly worked in a limited range of occupations and industries, focused predominantly on unskilled work or domestic service, but with demand from the manufacturing industries growing with the needs of the war, women were increasingly drawn into heavy industry and manufacturing roles.

The influx of female workers into industries and roles previously occupied by men raised a number of serious questions. The changes in the workforce within existing industries, and the development of purpose-built factories, such as those at Gretna and Georgetown, also caused concerns over employee welfare. As a result, the government drew up a series of guidelines that covered all aspects of work from hours of work, sickness, industrial diseases, provision of food and washing facilities through to the role of welfare officers. The duties of the welfare supervisor also included advising workers on sources of recreation and education within or near to their workplaces, in order to encourage rest and relaxation outside of work hours or during breaks. A letter to the manager of the NPF at Cardonald from the Ministry of Munitions highlights the need to provide male workers with access to football pitches in order to encourage them to play during their meal hours 'with a desire to stop the men passing their time gambling'. The active promotion of sport, and in particular football, as an antidote to antisocial or disruptive behaviour amongst workers is particularly significant. This fragmentary evidence, suggests that football was also formally promoted to female workers, and consequently evidence shows that women within these factories did start to play the game and even form teams from relatively early in their wartime employment.

Within the press, at both local and national level in Scotland, the emergence of the female footballer or 'munitionette' foot-baller was establish in the first half of 1917 and continued for the duration of the war. *The Dundee People's Journal* noted that,

> Some of our female munition workers are becoming keen devotees of football. On Magdalen Green way several of them can be seen nightly playing vigorously, attired in the garb which has become so familiar in the case of females since the outbreak of war. Some of them are very adept at the game, and can dodge their male opponents with remarkable dexterity.

The first recorded match between two women's war work teams was in May 1917, when two teams from the Mossend National Projectile Factory played against each other during a charity sports day held at Shawfield, in aid of the H L I Prisoners of War Fund. The eleven-a-side match was played between two teams from the same factory, 'Miss Somerville's Team' (Day Shift) and 'Miss Crawford's Team' (Night Shift). A crowd of

10,000 attended the sports day, which included over twenty events, yet the women's game was highlighted in several reports of the day, suggesting that it was popular.

By June, games were appearing with regularity at workplace sports events in Glasgow and its surrounding areas. The women's games were even, in some cases, being singled out for promotion in advance. As the *Motherwell Times* noted, in its only promotion of the forthcoming National Projectile Factory Sports Day, 'Are you near Fir Park tomorrow? Take the wife with you to see the lady footballers'.

Teams emerged from Government munitions factories such as Mossend, Georgetown and Cardonald, but there were also teams at shipbuilders Harland & Wolff and John Brown and Company, while other manufacturing industries such as Singers and textile manufacturers like Brothock and Alma Mills in Arbroath also fielded teams. Teams from Westburn Foundry, Beardmore's Parkhead Forge, Keith & Blackman at Arbroath, and other foundries were well represented. Teams that emerged from the industrial heartlands of the West and East of the Scottish Central Belt, centred around Glasgow and Edinburgh. There were however also a number of teams in the Dundee and Arbroath areas.

Teams were made up of women employed in the factories and mills they played for. One such team which emerged was from the Scottish Filling Factory (NFF), Georgetown, Houston, Renfrewshire. The NFF was opened in 1916, built as a response to the 1915 shell crisis. Georgetown, named after Lloyd George, consisted of two factories, known as No 1 and No 2, which were focused on assembling and filling quick-firing ammunition and breech-loading shell cartridges of varying sizes. At the peak of the war it was employing around 12,000 employees, the majority of whom were women.

The factory offered its employees a range of activities including football. Five-a-side matches for both male and female employees were a regular feature of the annual sports days, and from this, we can assume that a selection was made for the factory team. The workplace magazine, the *Georgetown Gazette*, noted in early 1918 that the girls' team was run by Mr Rankin (General Offices, Shell Factory) and Mr Hunter (Trolley Office, Cartridge Factory), while the team were coached by William Barr. The team were well regarded by the factory, articles in the *Gazette* noted that they 'were proving themselves no mean experts at the game' and 'after some further polishing the team should, we think, rank as one of the strongest of its kind'. Coaching suggests that the women were keen to play the game seriously and well. Indeed, articles in the works newspaper demonstrate that the team played matches regularly in various locations, mainly against other national projectile factories such as that at Cardonald, which had three women's teams. They took part in the Scottish Ladies Football Championship in July 1917 at Clyde Football Club Sports, against teams from other National Projectile Factories.

In the past, there had been a mixture of interest and antagonism towards female football players. However, because they raised significant amounts of money for charities, public matches were encouraged during the war. In addition to being enjoyable, going to these games was considered by some as patriotic since the gate proceeds went towards supporting regional or, more frequently, military charities. So instead of playing for themselves, the women were playing for the greater good. As this journalist in the *Daily Record* nicely summarises:

> Female football – we are to have 'some' at Shawfield
> on Saturday. The only excuse for it is that it may add a
> few pounds to a fund to assist H.L.I. prisoners of war.

While attendance was good, reporting of the matches themselves varied considerably in tone regarding the skills of the players and their understanding of the game as these two quotes from matches played only a few days apart in the west of Scotland demonstrate:

> Members of the fair sex have taken the place of the men in the factories, they have yet to acquire a few hints in the art of football.
>
> The feature of the afternoon's sport was the ladies' football match, Mile-End v. Mossend. The play was a revelation, the ladies being surprisingly clever in controlling the ball, while in front of goal the marksmanship was much admired.

In February 1918, the *Beardmore News*, the workplace newspaper of the Beardmore factories, advertised a forthcoming 'Grand Ladies' Football Match – England versus Scotland' at Celtic Park in Glasgow on 2 March. In reality, the teams were not national selections but rather teams selected from employees at munitions factories, Vickers-Maxim in Barrow-in-Furness and Beardmore's Parkhead Forge in Glasgow.

The match was hugely popular, with an estimated crowd of 15,000 attending. One match report noted that,

> On arrival at Celtic Park one thing was very noticeable. There were hundreds of soldiers and sailors clamouring for admission to view what they called 'the finest bob's worth of their lives.' All were wearing red or blue ribbons, showing which team they intended to support.

Cars conveying Sir William Beardmore, who would kick off the match, Lady Beardmore and their guests were driven to the athletics track at the edge of the pitch to the excitement of the crowd. England quickly took the lead scoring a goal within minutes of kick-off; by half-time, the score was England–3 Scotland–0. Half-time entertainment was provided by Mr Handiford and his comedy donkey act, followed by the Queen's Park Loco Silver Prize Band. England went on to win four goals to nil. Over £500 were raised for the Glasgow Infirmaries at the match, the equivalent of approximately £31,500 today. A return game was played on 23 March in Barrow-in-Furness in front of 5,000, ending in a 2–2 draw.

During the First World War, women played organised football on a regular basis in teams. Teams sprang up all over Scotland, frequently with local clusters growing in specific areas. Almost all of these teams originated from factories that produced items for the war and had a large number of female employees. There are still many gaps in our knowledge of women's football during this time, but there is evidence that shows for the first time that women's football existed across Scotland during the First World War.

NOTE:
This essay has been developed from recent research and a FIFA/CIES sponsored project mapping women's football in Scotland between 1880–1939.

PHENOMENAL

Julie McNeill

They were munitionettes,
canary girls and footballers
taking the spaces
vacated by lovers,

brothers, fathers.
Commentators said
they played '*with vigour
and remarkable dexterity*',

the same dexterity
that turned skin yellow
or brought them out of life
to fuel a war that wasn't theirs.

They saw wee Josie
chip the whole day shift
and dink the ball
into the waiting mouth

of the goal. Phenomenal
women, strong, sinewy,
pacy. In extraordinary times,
they ran that line together.

'LACE UP OUR BOOTS'

Paul Beeson & Bruce Strachan

THE FOLLOWING LYRICS are from the play 'Sweet F.A.' written by Paul Beeson and Bruce Strachan. Inspired by true events, 'Sweet F.A.' tells the vibrant story of one women's factory football team from Fountainbridge, Edinburgh, their friendships, loves, losses, and battles with their fierce rivals from Leith. 'Sweet F.A'. is an original play with music from This Is My Story Productions. It premiered to great reviews at the 2021 Edinburgh Festival Fringe. The script is published by Tippermuir Books (2022).

All: We toil on the work line to help fight the Hun,
            While the boys on the front line are having their fun,
            We take to the football fields, playing our game,
            They march into battle, but soon they'll come hame.

            We're doin' our bit, tae help win the war,
            Picked up the slack and discovered much more,
            We pull on our strips now, as eager recruits,It's time
            for us women to lace up our boots!

            We welcome our rivals, with arms open wide,
            Then send them packing, by tanning their hide,
            We work hard and play hard, remember our name,
            Don't try to tell us it's only a game!

            We're doin' our bit, tae help win the war,
            Picked up the slack and discovered much more,
            We pull on our strips now, as eager recruits
            It's time for us women to lace up our boots.
            Come on the NBR!

'Winning Working Women'

All: (*Singing*) We're aw women, working the war line
We're aw women working over-time
We're aw women, playing 'til full time
We're aw women, mighty Scottish quines

We're aw women, working the war line
We're aw women working over-time
We're aw women, playing 'til full time
We're aw women, mighty Scottish quines

Winning working women won't you hear what we've tae say
We work our hands unto the bones, for a quarter less in pay
We started our own football teams and showed them how to play
But when we ask for equal rights we're given Sweet FA

All: (*Spoken*) Welcome to Tynecastle!

Helen: Home of Heart of Midlothian Football Club!

Alice: It's 1915.

Daisy: Our boys in maroon finished the season second to Glasgow Celtic.

Harry: Oh, they were gutted no tae win the league after winning 19 of the opening 21 games.

Mo: But 13 players volunteered tae fight in France.

Lil: They were the talk o' the toon…

Daisy: But that's a story for another time …

Helen: This is our story. The story of women's football.

Reenie: Now, I ken what yer thinking.

Lil: Women didnae play football!

Harry: They're busy having bairns, keeping hoose and knowing their place.

All: But play they did!

(*Singing*) We're aw women, working like men folk
We're aw women, we're aw in the same boat
We're aw women, 'Equal Rights' – (Ha ha) Good joke!
We're aw women, all we're asking for's the vote!

Winning working women, won't you hear what we've tae say
We've gained a shade of yellow skin, lost fingers, hair and taes,
But apparently we're 'far too frail' for that fitba' game to play
You take our graft, and take our limbs, and give us Sweet FA

Helen: (*Spoken*) It was the most popular game for a while. Until the Football Authorities stepped in.

Suddenly the WOMEN become the SFA: LORD SCUNTHORPE, LORD DUNDEE, SECRETARY WATT, ABERCROMBIE, BUCHANAN AND CAMPBELL. They produce voting paddles that say 'AYE' on one side and 'NAY' on the other.

Lord Scunthorpe: All those in favour of stopping the women's game?

Each member raises his voting paddle to show 'AYE' and responds, apart from LORD DUNDEE.

All: Aye!

Lord Scunthorpe: Those against?

LORD DUNDEE raises his paddle to show 'NAY'.

Lord Scunthorpe: Are you sure? Perhaps you'd like to reconsider your vote, Lord Dundee?

They all turn and look at LORD DUNDEE, who sheepishly turns his paddle round.

Lord Scunthorpe: Resolution is hereby adopted. This, gentlemen, will put an end to this veritable curse!

All: Huzzah!

The WOMEN become themselves once more.

Helen: Who'd have thought the footballing authorities could be corrupted like that?

All: (*Singing*) We're aw women, football daft and crazy
We're aw women, we'd play fae Perth to Paisley
We're aw women, united we will stand
We're aw women, but the blazers want us banned

Winning working women won't you hear what we've tae say
We work our hands unto the bones, for a quarter less in pay
We started our own football teams and showed them how to play
But when we ask for equal rights we're given…
We're given…
Sweet FA!

UNTITLED POEM

Richard Ross

The English girls in jersey blue
Looked tidy, smart, and braw,
And showed their Scotch sisters
They were champions o' the baw.
All honour to these girls,
In a clever style they won,
They fairly beat the Scotch team
By four goals to one.

Let's hope the day may come,
When with pride it may be said,
The highest honours are being won
By the girls in jersey red.
So dinna be doonhearted,
But cheer up and come awa,
You yet may snatch the laurels
From those champions o' the baw.

Beardmore News, 19 March 1918

THE INTERNATIONAL (HOME)

Hamish MacDonald

A roar erupting into Glasgow skies
Miss Devlin leads her team to the field
thousands watch from Celtic Park's pavilion or stands
with colours pinned to lapels for the jerseys they will cheer
scarlet for Scotland, light blue for England
though they might have been remembrance ribbons
for those absent
the silent shadows in the crowd.

The 'munitionettes' taking the field of play
freed for this day from the heat and noise of machine shops
or daily grind with hammer, file, dwang, tap
assembling Howitzers and tanks
packing shells with TNT that turned the workers' skin
parchment yellow
sending more firepower to that unplayable surface
of the Western Front
where it seemed the final whistle would never come.

Servicemen watched from the crowd
on leave or invalided out
following the flight of the ball that it might distract them
from nightmares of death and destruction
the thought of going back to that.

At break time in the Parkhead ironworks
shouts of women had been heard, running feet on cobbles
the dunt of leather baw on brickwork
new industrial skills transferred from hand to foot
teams and contests sprang up, promising players emerged
and so to this international

Beardmores of Glasgow against Vickers of Barrow
Scotland versus England
raising spirits of the nation, funds for the Glasgow infirmaries.

The English girls showed fleet of foot
besting their hosts by three at half-time
a comeback out of the question
with stalwart centre half and captain Devlin
crocked at two goals down
but still the Scottish women rallied
a break on the left wing and cross into the box
attempts not enough to breach the England goal
another conceded
but sill enough to raise an almighty roar
until it would end that day
Celtic Park, Saturday 2nd March 1918
Scotland nil England four.

THE INTERNATIONAL (AWAY)

Hamish MacDonald

Rallied under the girders of Glasgow Central
resolved to avenge their defeat of two weeks before

the 10 am locomotive crossed the river
smoking Clydeside slipping to the distance
thistles bristling at feet
the claws of the lion tearing at hearts.

Railway miles passed
by farmland and pithead
discussing tactics and possible chinks in the armour of the

opposition
approaching rounded mountains with cloud shadows
Mr Taylor announced they would soon be over the
    Beattock Summit
changing at Carlisle
the strange sensation of that first time on English soil.

To the Friday reception at Barrow
and evening visit to the cinema where
pictures of Vickers' Celtic Park success were triumphantly
    screened
a further incentive to settle the score on the morrow.

With Devlin again leading out
gleg and gallus the Scottish eleven took the field
transformed from the previous encounter
until, 10 minutes in
Renwick picks up a well-timed pass from the right
Renwick to McLeish...McLeish to Renwick
the Vickers' defence pulled this way and that
the ball in the England net
Devlin adding a second with Vickers' munitionettes
stung into action
replying just before half-time.

It was a Beardmore's victory that might have been
but for that unfortunate handball and penalty decision
resulting in a 2–2 draw
and though not disputed on the field
would form the main topic of discussion and frustration
among other talking points and analysis
on the long journey home in darkness
by farmsteads, villages, towns and cities
with their empty rooms
where many would never be coming back.

THE GRETNA GIRLS

Stuart Kenny

6% petroleum jelly
42% nitroglycerine
52% collodion
kick-off, and play back to the midfield custodian

55% possession, on top are the B-Shift

Outside the factories, workers let minds drift
to a world where defence and attack
still means strikers versus full backs;
you get little time to relax – and none to be lazy
making the devil's porridge for the Royal Navy.
1–0 at half-time
across the country a boom in women's clubs
who'd play ball to stay fit
then trade football shirts for factory scrubs.

2–1 at the whistle
in the shadow of the largest munitions factory in the world,
home to 30,000 workers and almost half of them girls;
most under eighteen and most working class,
finding solace in a break on a pitch, and a well placed pass.

Game's over, Jessie. Time to make the next batch,
then Brunton Park next week for a charity match;
Carlisle Munition vs The Gretna Girls, and won't it be fun,
but first there's cordite to be made – and a war to be won.

EFFIE MACLEOD IS NO LONGER AVAILABLE

Hugh McMillan

In 1980 we set off
with our brand
new Video Cameras
to record the last
of the munitionettes.
One was taken ill immediately,

the next, Mrs Graves,
stoically received our tripod
in her pristine front room.
'I wis a hame loving lassie
steyed wi ma ma and dad
luvved the extra cash.

Met my late husband
he was a polisman.'
This was not what we wanted,
Joyce and I, young fervent
history teachers
on the hunt for tales

of drink and sexuality,
free girls making the most
of their freedom.
At last after a custard
cream she conceded:
'Ah mind some frae Ireland,

worse, the islands, they
were wild as Rannoch,
they were aff their heids
the stuff they did –
drinking, hijacking trains,
playing fitba like men.

It was a national scandal
aw hushed up cos o the war.
Yon Effie Macleod wis
fae Raasay, spent mair
time in jankers than in the sheds.
She steys in Vancouver Avenue.

Ye ken whit the Food Train
brings her?
A bottle o vodka a day.
Hijacking trains!
Playing Fitba like men!
Jankers! Vodka!

This was more like it.
We went to the pub,
drank beer, plotted
a visit to Effie: Was this
the centre half of the legendary
Gretna Girls team

who hammered the Carlisle
Munitionettes at Brunton Park?
As we were packing
our equipment we heard news
that Mrs Graves had died –
a heart attack.

There go the angels of death
joked the Jannie as we left.
Her's was a council house,
neat curtains and a ginger cat
on the step and a note on the door.
'Effie Macleod is no longer available for
interviews.'

A GOAL OF THEIR AMBITION

Onlooker
A Proposal to Ban Women Players Has Been
Placed Before the Football Association

It's a sad world, my masters;
So wherefore scorn the fair,
Who want to chase a ball around,
And sprawl and maul on muddy ground,
And drive away dull care?

Tis true they meet disasters,
While rude onlookers roar;
But merriment is scarce to-day,
And, if you ban their football, they
Will only kick the more!

NOTE:
Anonymous poem published in the *Daily Record*, 6 December 1921, one
day after the ban was introduced in England.

TO BAN OR NOT TO BAN:
A Brief History Of The 'Ban' And The Lifting Of The Ban In Scotland
Fiona Skillen & Karen Fraser

THE 5TH OF DECEMBER 2021 marked the centenary of the introduction of a 'ban' on women's football by the Football Association (FA) in England. The ban prevented women's matches from taking place on football grounds owned by members of the FA. It also prevented any male players or officials from participating in any way with the playing of matches by women. In doing this, the FA were trying to stamp out the women's game which had grown considerably during the First World War. They argued that football was 'unsuited' to delicate female bodies and could cause serious physical and psychological harm. They also argued, based on little evidence, that the women's game in England was corrupt. The ban was to stay in place until 1970.

In Scotland, the Scottish Football Association (SFA) did not formally introduce a ban at this point, but they did to all intents and purposes try to limit where women could play and the involvement of members in arranging matches. This had a similar effect to the ban in England, making it more difficult for teams to find pitches and public support. As a consequence of the attitudes of the football authorities, many of the wartime teams which had continued in the year or so after the war disbanded. One exception to this was Rutherglen Ladies FC, who were founded in 1921 and went on to be the leading team in interwar Scotland. More formalised attempts at a ban in Scotland were introduced by the SFA after the Second World War and remained in place until 1974.

As the 1970s dawned, across Europe women footballers started to demand that their national football associations improved equalities and lifted restrictions on their game. In

June 1971, at its Monte Carlo Congress, the Union of European Football Associations (UEFA) urged its member nations to lift the restrictions imposed on women's football, recognise the game and take control of women's football. While this was a positive move, it was unfortunately less about encouragement of the women's game and more about ensuring that the national associations had influence and control over the way in which the women's game developed as they were concerned to preserve the amateur status of the game.

The UEFA resolution in which member associations agreed to take charge of the control of women's football in their countries, was agreed by 31 votes to 1, with Scotland the lone dissenting voice. The SFA were unconvinced and decided to take the UEFA resolution as guidance rather than a ruling and refused to lift the restrictions on women's football in Scotland. There is no clear information about why the SFA defied the ruling with records merely stating that they disagreed with the proposal. The following year, in an interview about the first women's international match, Willie Allen, the SFA chief executive, provided an insight when he stated that the SFA did not approve of ladies playing football.

Exasperation with the attitude of the SFA led those involved in the women's game in Scotland to recognise the need for better central co-ordination of both the game and the lobbying of the SFA for recognition. This led to the formation of the Scottish Women's Football Association (SWFA) by six teams on 17 September 1972. As part of their campaign to show their serious intentions and to promote women's football, the SWFA created the first official women's football league with twelve teams. It supported several competitions and organised two international matches between 1972 and August 1974. The SWFA hoped that the league, competitions and international matches would indicate the serious attitude of the SWFA and be of support in their bid for recognition.

The SFA continued to hold its position despite growing participation and lobbying by the SWFA. There was little indication that this approach was working and so the decision made by the SFA in August 1974 came as a surprise:

> Women's Football (Item 70. Executive and General Purposes Committee): It was agreed to give recognition to women's football. (SFA Minutes, 29 August 1974).

The short SFA minute gives no background to the decision. There is a possibility that influenced by changes in wider society, combined with the resistance of the women playing and the evolving infrastructure, the SFA simply changed their mind. This is, however, unlikely, given the lack of support for women's football from the SFA across the next twenty years. It is far more likely that the force for change came from outside the SFA. There is speculation that one driver for change was a threat of sanctions (potential limitations on participation in European football and the imposition of fines) from UEFA, that might have had a negative impact on the men's game, although to date it has not proved possible to verify this. Equally probable is the potential impact from the impending Sex Discrimination Act 1975. While the Act exempted sport's organisations from aspects of the equality legislation, the hand of the SFA was likely forced by Section 29 which prohibited discrimination against women with regard to the provision of goods and services. This effectively ended the SFA's ability to demand that its member clubs forbade women the use of their facilities and for officials to refuse to officiate a women's match. Given the timing of the decision, it is likely that the combination of a potential UEFA fine and the introduction of anti-discrimination legislation brought about the recognition of women's football.

This minute ended the restrictions placed on the women's

game decades before and brought Scotland in line with other members of UEFA. This decision meant that women's teams now had the potential to use the facilities and resources of SFA member football clubs and engage the services of licensed officials.

The SFA's reluctant recognition of women's football in 1974 was undoubtedly a significant marker in the development of the game but did not herald respect or support from the dominant football community. There was little material change to the experiences of women playing across the next twenty years.

This was because the male football community were assisted by prevailing societal gender stereotypes to support their endeavours to limit the extent to which women's football developed. Although there continued to be little support for or encouragement to women's football, there was no public outcry about the overt sexism and discrimination taking place as most feminist activism did not view sport as a site for action. The result was that women in football continued to challenge for equality of opportunity on their own, with little support from the wider women's community.

However, the fact that women's football was recognised does not mean that everything was positive. Following the lifting of restrictions in August 1974, the SWFA with minimal resources, strove to organise domestic and international football, meet the needs of its members and endeavour to promote, develop and grow the women's game. The lack of resources seriously impacted the ability to undertake this work and to become established as a recognised and respected governing body. To address this, the SWFA sought to achieve affiliation to the SFA to assist its efforts to grow the game. However, SWFA endeavours were thwarted by the SFA and the insistence that the number of members (individual and team) was the most important factor in the decision to grant affiliation. The SFA were not interested in the ever-growing number of women playing outside the SWFA structures, this was about formal membership.

The SWFA believed that as a national organisation with ambitions for expansion, affiliation should not be based on numbers alone. The SFA declared, that to warrant affiliation, it required the SWFA to become more professional and gain more financial independence. This struggle continued for a further 24 years until in February 1998, it was announced that the SFA had accepted the recommendation of an Independent Review Commission and as a result the SWFA was granted affiliation. This was welcomed as affiliation meant that the SWFA could finally seek additional grants and longer-term sponsorship. There had been discussion about amalgamation but this never happened.

In June 2000, the SWFA held an extraordinary general meeting, which passed a resolution to turn the SWFA into a limited company. This transition happened in 2001 when the SWFA became the SWF (Ltd). The move established the SWF as a company that could enter into contracts in its own name (including employing staff), had the legal right to money it made from sales and keep its profits, was responsible for paying its own debts and liabilities and is responsible for its own actions. This confirmed the SWF as a separate entity from the SFA and prepared the way for it to grow and develop on its own terms, rather than seeking amalgamation.

THAT MAN

Ann Park

That man banned ma gran
he took away her ba'
denied her skill
imposed his will
and passed a man-made law.

Ma gran defied that man
his nonsense didnae faze her
she used a van
tae beat the ban
and get it up the blazer.

That man should carry the can
and make good reparations
for years of shame
on the beautiful game
support new generations.

A MOST UNSUITABLE GAME

Allan Gaw

You had me carrying shell casings in ten-hour shifts.
I wielded a heavy scythe in the sweating heat of
summer.
I worked the cleaver and the knife in your abattoir.
I dug and shovelled, carried and heaved but
Only now I am too delicate to play this game?

What has changed? What do you grey men fear now?
You say it's unseemly, a cheap burlesque for prying eyes.
But at the same time you insult me, saying I have made
myself manly, devoid of delicacy and feminine finesse.
Alluring and repulsive? Surely I cannot be both.

So then you claim I will damage myself beyond repair,
That I lack the strength, the frame to cope.
You call medical witnesses to support your cause.
And worse, you conclude, I will squander my fertility,
That I will injure that which most makes me a woman.

Is that the crux? Is that my role, now the men are home?
That I must put away my overalls, put down my tools,
And I must leave the game to them and only
Dream of goals scored and sweet victories won,
Before retreating into your homes to be silent.

Silent but working, lifting, cooking, scrubbing, and
Giving life to heroes, without ever being one myself.

THE GIRLS OF TAIN LAUNDRY 1940

Lynsey Gilmour

I knew most of them,
Much later, when the glow
Had dimmed from young faces,
When white hair, set and curled
Ready for bowling club bingo, or Guild gossip,
Had replaced the hairnets and
Wisps spilling from the confines
Of overly ambitious kirby grips.

But the ready warmth and friendship,
That seem to spill like sooty stains
From the confines of a grainy photograph, I know.
And I recognise the shoulders raised and rounded,
Ready to let forth the throatiest laughter,
I recognise the fortitude
Of young women finding fun and friendship,
Together on the pitch while their world tilts on its axis.

Long after June of 1940,
When almost every boy in Tain had been taken,
Forsaken on a beach in France.
Long after they'd been found again.
When sweethearts had become wives,
When the girls of the Laundry
Had become mothers, grandmothers,
There was little left to tell of the war at home,

But the determined image of eleven girls,
Friends, sisters, colleagues,
Arms around one another,
Squinting at the sun,
Refusing to wait for better days,
When a better day might be made on the pitch.
Tells a story I recognise,
Of women I was proud to know.

GRANNY READER

AKA Sadie Smith

Eddi Reader

Her face beamed with smiles and red broken veins as she
lowered her face to talk to me gently.
In the scullery where I would always find her.
Scraping carrots into juice, offering me a sip.
Or she would lead me towards the back of the door where she
kept her treasure bag stretching heavy, full of oranges.
These things were important.
She was smaller than her children but I was even smaller and I
would tug her apron for any delicious thing she might offer.
The famous soup was all I would eat.
She didn't shout at me to eat like the other grown-ups.
Ever gentle, ever smiling, ever there in that crammed-in
kitchen.
A sanctuary of warmth, her domain where I would find her
loving kindness.
A constant peace amongst the loud, party loving, masculine
dominated, Ruchill flat.
'One Nine Five
Bilsland Drive'.
A poem of a place that was my dad's family home.

That is the only memory I own of my namesake Sedania
'Deana' Evans Reader (née Smith). A white haired, smiling
woman. Her face so close to mine I saw the hundreds of tiny
red veins which gave her skin a glow of crimson.
That memory and the memory of one Glasgow night in my
dad's car when, from the window, I saw them all descending
the hospital steps,
Wet with rain and tears. Followed by the news that she had gone.

I was seven or eight years old.

Later when I was told the story of her footballing genius, one of her surviving children mentioned that, when they were wee and playing football in the back courts, others remarked:

'Ach! Yur good son, but no as good as yur mother!'

They never understood what was meant by those remarks.
They never knew she achieved greatness as an athletic footballer.
I'm not sure her children even were aware of how involved in football she was in her younger days.

Today I remember those scullery moments alone with her and imagine while she was encouraging me to drink her delicious carrot juice, before pouring it all into a bubble pot of goodness, she was quietly remembering scoring glorious goals.

I come from great stock.
Thank you Granny.

Love Sedania 'Eddi' Reader

SECTION ENDNOTES

1   Robert Chambers, *Domestic Annals of Scotland from the Reformation to the Rebellion of 1745* (Edinburgh, 1858), p448; 'Waddle and Lamming toune,' *Statistical Account of Scotland, XVI* (Edinburgh: 1795), p823; 'Lesmahagow', *Hamilton Advertiser*, 30 August 1873, p2.

2   George Imbert in England, Select Births and Christenings, 1538–1975, 30 November 1822, Saint Leonard's, Shoreditch, London.

3   1861 Scotland Census Glasgow Barony; ED: 90; p4, ln11; Roll: CSSCT1861_109 & 1871 England Census Class: RG10; Piece: 4009; Folio: 5; p6; GSU roll: 846105.

4   'Athletic Jottings', *Glasgow Evening News and Star*, 27 April 1881, p3.

5   'Females in the Field', *Blackburn Standard*, 28 May 1881, p5; 'Whitsuntide at Halifax', *Bradford Daily Telegraph*, 7 June 1881, p4.

6   'Football,' *Manchester Evening News*, 21 June 1881, 3, 'Lady Football Players – Last match To-night', *Liverpool Echo*, 28 June 1881, p1.

7   'Women at Football', *St James Gazette*, 28 November 1885, p6; 'Lady Footballers in Stockport', *Stockport Advertiser*, 7 May 1920, p5; 'The Ladies Football Match', *Hull Daily Mail*, 11 April 1887, p4.

8   'A Skittish Young Lady at Southend', *Barking, East Ham & Ilford Advertiser*, 17 April 1897, p4.

9   'Music Hall And Theatrical Mems', *London and Provincial Entr'acte*, 4 December 1897, p10; 'New York Theatre', *New York Tribune*, 12 January 1908, p2.

10 'Mr Alec Payne', *Era*, 22 February 1890, p17.

11 'Ladies at Football', *Windsor and Eton Express*, 7 December 1895, p3; 'Echo v Express Charity Match', *Liverpool Daily Post*, 27 December 1892, p6.

12 'The "Original" Lady Footballers', *Birkenhead News*, 11 January 1896, p2.

13 'The Lady Footballers in Distress', *Stonehaven Journal*, 16 July 1896, p2.

14 'Skaters Carnival at Merton', *Wimbledon News*, 9 March 1912, p8.

15 'Glasgow Pantomime Girls Look "Chic" as Footballers', *Daily Record*, 18 February 1914, p8; 'Lady Variety Artiste's Football Match for Charity', *Leeds Mercury*, 7 March 1914, p6.

For The Love Of The Game

In this section are poems and short essays that provide an insight into why women play football despite all the challenges faced by them. These range from bans and abuse, lack of support and facilities, to needing to carve out time away from all their other responsibilities to take part in the beautiful game. They do it for the simple reason that they love football.

WHO DARES?

Julie McNeill

I'd have given anything to see them
become champions of the world,
Sadie and the ladies
dodging, feinting, swerving
round the Dick Kerr Girls.

They showed them how it's done,
shimmying past the cross bald men
who declared it was wrong
for anyone to dare
to look at women footballers.

They kept the head
and stood up tall
when bans, fans, associations
told them to stick
to *folk football*:

you know, the games
where men
chaperone, tie their hands
behind their backs
let the ladies score,

then having chivalrously lost,
take back the ball. This stadium
saw the beginning
of the end to that.

These girls were women
worth watching.

HAD I KNOWN THEN, WHAT I KNOW NOW, THINGS MIGHT BE DIFFERENT; AND YET, I WOULDN'T CHANGE IT FOR THE WORLD

Lindsay Hamilton
Tour Guide and Business Owner at
The Glasgow Football Tour

HINDSIGHT is an indelibly powerful, unavoidable, part of life. A couple of years back, I had the honour of being accompanied by the great Pat Woods, a real Scottish footballing anorak of a particular Celtic vintage. I told him, as we walked past the enveloped and iconic Celtic Park wrapped in green parcel detailing legends of the past which read, 'Where Legends Are Made', that I actually once played for this great club and played out on that hallowed turf. 'I wasn't very good', I added, then continued, 'I didn't play very well, or for many minutes, let alone games'. Pat replied, quickly & assertively, 'Every player, every single player, who plays for Celtic Football Club is special – you are no exception to this'.

Now, I could certainly think of many a player who played in the Hoops who wasn't particularly special, but I'm not writing this essay about Shane Duffy, it's about women's fitba. It's about my life in football, I guess.

I have played the game since I was a little girl attending St Ambrose Primary School in the Milton (North Glasgow). There wasn't a day that went by when I wouldn't receive a chap at the door from my big pal and next door neighbour, Sean, to ask, 'You coming out for a game?' The answer to that question, you ask? 'Is the Pope Catholic?' I was there, every single day, out playing with my pal; mud coating every stitch of clothing I owned.

I still remember telling him that I had made it big and was going to earn a weekly wage playing for Arsenal Ladies FC.

I had a trial and my daft Da told me that'd I'd likely get a signing bonus. Gullible wee Lindsay, who had a lot to learn, sprinted next door to tell her big pal and to celebrate. What did we do to celebrate? Played football in the back garden! Not a single care in the world. As far as I was concerned I was about to buy my Ma a new house with my earnings. Jeez oh!

I was signed by Arsenal and had to retract my statement to everyone, their granny and their granny's dug that I told I was going to earn big bucks playing seven-a-side football for Arsenal Ladies. Sake John! However, my time there didn't last long. Arsenal Ladies, playing out of the East End at Crownpoint, were bought over by local side, Celtic Football Club. I still have nightmares about that trial day at Barrowfield. I remember for the first time seeing that iconic sign, 'STAY OFF THE GRASS'. I walked up to that place thinking of Larsson, Tommy Twists, Jinky and Jock. I could barely breathe. 'This was my big chance', I thought! I was twelve years old. Hindsight, by Christ! At the end of the session, with what seemed like 100,000 girls all trying to get into the Hoops starting XI, we were split into the home and away dressing rooms. I was in the away. It was there that they told us, 'Unfortunately, you were unsuccessful this time'. It was brutal. My dreams – shattered! I'm laughing as I write this. It's entirely as it seemed at the time but my goodness young Lindsay, give it time. You're only twelve once.

I moved on to pastures new. Played football for various different teams, including Airdrie, Cumbernauld Cosmos, Celtic (got all the way to the reserves by the way), United Glasgow and BSC. I did so until I was 27 back in 2021. I'd had enough. Want to know why? It made me miserable. I never understand when people say playing football gives them this great relief; like nothing else in the world exists. For me, and I should most likely invest in therapy, football amplified all my issues. My self-confidence, or lack thereof, was magnified. It's like my own brain was punishing me, cruelly, over most of the

90 minutes I ever played from teenage years all the way through to adulthood. So why did I play as long as I did? Well I was semi-good at it. I didn't have anything really that I was semi-good at after school ended. Above all that, I formed some tremendous relationships and met some of life's genuinely most wonderful people. But internally, I had to stop for fear it would be the death of me quite frankly. You're probably wondering at this point where this is all going, but I promise you it'll come full circle. Please, pop the kettle on, grab a cup of tea and pull up a pew.

Throughout my entire life, I believed, strongly, that I never really had, or indeed found, my place in football. I couldn't see what piece I was in the jigsaw. I had tried my hand at coaching, done some administrative work, and played for as long as my poor mental health would allow. Then, the pieces all fell into place. University wasn't easy for me. I was devoid of a large group of friends until my third year and felt entirely lonely. Wow! I'm painting a sad, sorry picture. However, every cloud has a silver lining and mine was soon to come in the shape of Hampden Park, and the Scottish Football Museum. In my final year, my dissertation focused on William Struth of Rangers Football Club. I used the museum to research the football club, and his life and fell completely head over heels with the place. 'You mean to tell me, you get to speak to people from all over the world about football, all day long, and you get paid for it?' My head was turned! This was it. This was my place. I immediately made it known to Colin, who was the museum manager at the time, that I was looking to become a tour guide. He agreed to take me on and from then on it all suddenly clicked into place. 'You're the wee lassie that does the stadium tours?' That's me! It still fills me with pride eight years on since I started out.

I've found throughout my life that being lower than a worm's tit certainly has its advantages. For all I have struggled, I've done a lot of cool things in football and the coolest thing yet was set in stone when I decided to set up my own football tourism business in January 2019. The idea hit me between the eyes one day sitting in Hampden Park. Armed with a single sheet of paper from the nearby printer and a pencil I wrote down every little thing I thought I might need to kick start this new, exciting venture. I went home and told my Ma, 'I'm going to start a business', she replied, 'Great! So you should'. And that was me.

The title of this essay is 'Had I Known Then, What I Know Now, Things Might be Different; and Yet, I Wouldn't Change It For the World'. What I know now is that the women's game, to my absolute delight, has come on leaps and bounds. There are players now, my age and younger, who can be paid as full-time professionals – as they should – and make a real career out of the game. Scotland women's international fixtures, domestic league games in the SWPL and domestic cup semi-finals and finals are breaking attendance records and improving season upon season. BBC Scotland's *Sportscene* are showing a weekly highlight show while ALBA and BBC Sport Scotland are giving fans like me the opportunity to watch their heroes on their phones, laptops and TVs from the comfort of their home. Could that have been me? If I had sought the help of a therapist, cut down on the fry-ups and fast food and not discovered alcohol at seventeen years of age then yeah perhaps. But truth be told, I wasn't fond of working out – in fact, I hate it. I try my best but it's a real pain in the backside. I often think now though, if I knew then that one day I could have been on *Sportscene*, played a competitive game at Celtic Park, Ibrox or Hampden, or perhaps even become a professional footballer – would I have put in more effort. Maybe? But, as I've said, hindsight is an indelibly powerful, unavoidable, part of life. The reality was, I didn't see a future in it at the time and in the long run it was not good for my wee head. If I'm being honest, it was never really my dream. I didn't know what my dream was until it struck me on the dome back in my single office bunk in the national stadium. The point I suppose I'm making is that as women, we can dream of a life in football. We can dream big. We can dream up any piece of the footballing jigsaw we want to be a part of. Had I known then that I could have potentially been a professional, lots of ifs, buts and maybes in there, would things have been different? Perhaps. But I wouldn't change it for the world. Why? Because I now have the opportunity to build a business that I know years from now will tell the story to may folk around the world of Glasgow City's origin, outside of their own stadium (which will come), as a club that has no affiliation to a men's side. I will tell folk about record-breaking attendances for women's games at Celtic Park, Ibrox and Hampden. We will shine a light on the positive future of this game for women and will no longer merely be defined by a ban, which while important, is not and never was the full story.

My place in football is to tell the world about Glasgow's unique football heritage and culture. Women's football is part of that. My story is part of that. And the world is going to know it.

BRAVE

Thomas Clark

The bravest player ah ever saw
Wisnae thon…ye ken the type;
Player, tap-soil, earth's core, baw,
Last tae sorry, first tae clype,

Screams at team-mates, referees,
Onybody that's in their road,
Flies at ankles, shinpads, knees,
Plays the gemme in psycho mode.

The bravest player wis aye, for me,
That lassie chyngin on her ain,
Thirteen, wan-quean corps d'esprit,
Tyin up her lion's mane,

Redd for aw the boys an das
Crowdin pitches, fower-five deep,
Jeerin every misplaced pass,
Mimin every mistimed leap;

But wance the snell rain stairts tae faw,
An they're aw aff, back hame tae chitter,
She'll still be oot there, weary, raw,
Teuch as blowster, stuir as watter.

If ah had been sae brave, nae braver,
Then, or noo…Let naebody claim
This luve wis meant for menfowk. Havers.
We're jist the players. She's the gemme.

BEING A FEMALE IN FOOTBALL
Isla Buchanan
Football Referee

I HAVE HAD an interest in football from a young age. I wanted a pair of football boots but my dad's answer was no, unless I joined a team. So, that night at the age of ten I got some new football boots and joined my local team which is where my love of football continued to grow.

I wanted to play football whenever I could: in the garden, after school as well as during school but this is where the barriers of being a female in football came into play. I wanted to play for the primary school team but I was told due to being a female I could only train with the team but couldn't play. It was something I pushed hard to change but sadly I still wasn't allowed.

Being female in a male-dominated environment has its challenges. I'd experienced it from playing and I now experience it from being a football referee. My grandad was a referee, that's how I got into it and I've never looked back. However, it wasn't easy at first: arriving at the location of the game prior to kick off was one of the most nerve-wracking experiences I've had. I remember most of the guys stopping their warm-up to look at me and all I could hear was, 'Is that a female referee?' I could feel them all staring.

Eventually, they got to know me and the local teams got used to me, however, it's not always been plain sailing. I have experienced a large number of sexist comments along the way which, I admit, have affected me mentally. Comments such as 'Women shouldn't be in football', 'Women shouldn't be referees' and 'You should be in the kitchen', to mention just a few.

Football and refereeing have allowed me to grow in confidence and become stronger as an individual. I'm forever proud to be a female in football.

SCORE

Janet Crawford

then come the back slaps
the high fives
the sideways nods of pride from the stand
– as mums and grannies clap –

whilst the younger girls sit as a team
watching each move, then cheer as one
and the energy flow moves on
lifting everyone

the team realising that this body of women,
    helps them all strive
to play both in and beyond any position
    put upon them in life
always looking up, defending each other and
the incoming ball
knowing a shout of hold, behind you or here
with a hand raised tall
helps us to move on beyond
where we think more than the ball might go.

SET THE STAGE

Julie McNeill

She dusts the dugout
and sharpens the sunlight,
dresses the white lines
with precision and formality.

She showcases the woodwork,
denier of dreams and maker of miracles,
and embraces the centre spot,
the site of all new beginnings.
While the
        clock
                still   ticks
the scales can still tip
and anything is possible.

Imprints and echoes below
do nothing to slow her progress.
Expectation and anticipation
are borne of what went before.

After the frost, a softening thaw
and, in time, once more
we'll hear the thunderous,
wondrous, fan-fuelled roar.

FITBA WITH MA MAW
Alistair Heather

SO, I TOOK MY MUM to her first Scottish women's football game. I did want to go with her but, between me and you, I had been struggling to get my usual Dundee United mates along to the women's matches. So, I had to recruit a new fitba pal to come along and keep me company, and my mum fit the bill. She grew up quite athletic, and played pub football. So, she understands the game.

We're both from Angus, and our region just got its first top-flight team: Montrose. They were playing Dundee United and I reckoned a mum-and-son trip to Links Park for a derby would be the perfect environment to mint a new United supporter.

It is so easy, as we get older and live in different towns, to go months without speaking. A United fixture in the diary would be a guarantee of a meet-up, a chance to get lunch, get a catch-up, and take in a game. Same as I know loads of my pals meet their dad for games, and seldom see them away from the stadium.

The December rain was absolutely sheeting the streets. I had the umbrella clutched an inch above our heads to limit the invitation of the wind to lift it. A rotten day. My socks were sodden by the time we'd settled into our seats under the roof of Links Park.

On the walk, I'd explained the derby backstory: United and Montrose were both in the lower reaches of the table and battling to get clear of relegation. Half a dozen players had left United to join the Montrose dressing room, after disputes with United's coaching team. In the first game of the season, Montrose won 3–2, their first win in the league.

'Alllllyyy calm the ham', mum said, embarrassed.

I'd boomed out a big 'MON UNITEEED' at kick-off.

The douce folk of Montrose had turned disapproving eyes towards me. I was about the only away fan.

Montrose took the lead. Neve Guthrie, a player synonymous with Dundee United since she joined as a teen in 2018, fired the shot home past her old team.

'Come on MONTROSE! Oh sorry', mum hushed herself.

She'd got swept away in the general cheer that greeted Guthrie's goal.

Damnit. Mum was meant to be a United fan.

But the Terrors were flailing. As the home side continued to build dominance, United got dirty. Their tackles nipped more ankle than ball. The tactics became simple hoof balls long up the pitch then our hard-running forwards being sicced on it.

My mum firmly disapproved, tutting every bad challenge. Against the run of play, United scored goals before and after the half-time. I'd barked my approval both times, and my mum had hushed me.

Mum practically skipped the walk home.

'I can't believe that. That lassie jumping up and scoring that header was amazing! I'll remember that forever.' Montrose had equalised in the 87th minute. A bitter pill.

Then Jade McClaren, one of the central midfield mainstays for United in seasons passed, popped up in the second minute of stoppage time to power home a header, and steal the game for Montrose. Bitter, bitter. Montrose won the game, and won my mum as a supporter.

Over a cup of tea at home, me and mum reviewed the day. The half-time scran and atmosphere got a thumbs-up. The weather a thumbs-down. Mum wasnae sure about the sheer physicality of the game; some of the kicks the young women were taking took her aback.

We've got a final derby, which with Montrose and United battling near the relegation zone should be a cracker. Me and my mum will get along to that, too. It's a home tie for me, so mum will come in on the train and I'll be in charge of sorting lunch, and we'll get a chance to hang out for an afternoon.

United lost their chance to claim my mum as a fan. A cement. But at least I've company for the derbies. We'd better win the next one.

JUIST NAW 1989

Keeks Mc

'Leuk at the state o you!
Ye fling like a wee girlie
Yer crap!'
Ah wisnae guid
tho Ah wantit tae be
...an it wis kis Ah wis a girl
No an inherent inleak o abeelity
but an imponed dearth o investment an ae
  owerplus o apathy
No fur aa
but siccarly maist
an shuirly in mid-class suburban Glesga
Ah mind it perqueerly
P5 it wis
whan the muckle heilan teacher
cam doon fae the big schuil
the recruiter fur the excitin sports
fitba, cammock an rugby
He speirt wha wantit tae list fur trainin
A wheen o laddies put thair haunds up
...an me an Esther
He notit the lads names than makkit tae leave
but in an early act o conterdiction
we yowtit
'whit aboot us?'
He teuk us ootside
an said three wee words
'Naw! Yer lassies'
shrugged an turnt his back
again wir quizzin
an wee disjaskit herts

WEE LASSIE IN THE BIG BOYS' WORLD

Cat Cochrane

She stood 4 foot 6 with her hands in the air.
the year the garden festival swept into town

The dilemma of the boys' 11-a-side
or the lassies' netball team
was *no* dilemma at all,
her wing attack days left
on squeaky gym hall floors

—as when Billy Mc, Big Rab
and Toe Poke Deek
picked you for their playground team,
gender wasn't the talking point

Trading skills in hockey cages
with ash-burnt knees,
white socks turnt orange from true grit,
her toughest decision was
Adidas Kick, or Puma Match
…once her parents saved up

When the day came to pull on the jersey,
down the left wing like a Tasmanian devil
with intent, she whipped in crosses
the speed of whippets across grassland

With shouts of *Tommy Boy*
from the sidelines, she was likened
to Jinky or Gordon Strachan in
both ginger and wee-ness,

man-made comparisons
—no female idols off the tongue
                        as there were none

The lads did weekly Boys' Brigade
reappearing with funny notions
about their *peepul* status in life,
parochial sparks that reared
against schools named after saints

For one season only
Mitre Deltas blootered about
in all weather kickabouts,
adrenalin pumped for matchday Fridays,
–her first sight of full lawn pitches
a mecca moment in time

On the weekends
she'd play out the back garden
—creating a World Cup for girls,
running on with number 11 on her back
representing a whole new nation,
a place for tiny heroines

Halcyon primary days slide tackled
into secondary semesters,
where PE teachers alluded to
hormonal intricacies the reason
boys and lassies
won't mix in the football team
With no designated girls' coach
they may as well have placed
a *do not enter* sign at the door

and a peg for her football boots
…before she'd even outworn them.

The Importance Of The Changing Room
Sam Milne
In Conversation With Karen Fraser

Introduction

Sam Milne, a Scottish Football Association (SFA) Club Development Officer, is very happy that women and girls in Scotland now have far more options to play football than they did until relatively recently. She believes that while women's football in Scotland is in a good place, especially for the younger generations coming through, players need to appreciate that this is not how it has always been. Those playing today should be aware of the history of the game and the lengths that women and girls would go to, to play football and hopes that books like this will provide that insight.

She also sees the need for the telling of a variety of stories from different perspectives as everyone has different experiences of involvement in football. In her view:

> We all have a different experience of it and it still impacts on our lives in so many ways, without playing professionally and without playing for a national team. People relate to different stories – so it is good to have a variety.

Sam's own story is one of a love of playing, a career in football development and a moment of revelation that led to an opportunity both for Sam to return to kicking a ball and opening up that opportunity to numerous other women with their own stories to tell. Together they are stories of the importance of the changing room.

Sam's Football Story

Sam's earliest memories of football are about watching her brother play football and finding a way to join in.

> I was about five or six and my brother played football but there was nothing for me to do so I just played on the sidelines, kicking the ball around, doing keepie-ups, tackling the subs, that type of thing and that was every Sunday.

She recalled people looking at her and wondering why they were staring, 'I realise now, it was because it was a girl playing football'.

At the time, Sam was not able to find a girls' team to play for, and played football with boys whenever she could. Things were not always easy though and one bad memory involves trials for her primary school football team. Sam recalled:

> I went along and I remember that I did well, scored loads of goals and thought I did well. Like all the boys I was so excited waiting for my name to be put up on the list to say whether you made the team or not. I did not make the team.

Sam said that her mum went to the school to tell them how disappointed she was and was told that Sam had been left out of the team because there were no toilets and so she could not get changed. The history of women's football in Scotland is full of tales of lack of facilities like changing rooms and the inventive way women and girls found to get ready for a match and Sam would have been up for this, but was not given the chance.

This setback did not deter Sam who said she never thought, 'I am not allowed to play this' and just accepted the situation, there was no football team for her that was just how it was. She just kept playing wherever and whenever she could. She played with a couple of boys' teams and in the park with friends when she could. When she was eleven, she signed for Dundee United ladies. This was the mid-1990s and the separation of women's and girls' football was still in its infancy.

Talking about that time, Sam said:

> I loved it, just loved it and I have the most supportive parents but back then it wasn't that it was discouraged but it wasn't encouraged either. They are so proud of me now but how different might it have been without, at that time, peer pressure to suggest that your daughter should not be playing a man's game.

In talking about her parent's support she added, 'It was looked on as a phase, but I am nearly 40 now and still love it so it's not a phase!'

Sam spent seventeen years playing league football, the majority in the Premier League with Forfar Farmington. Playing football was a way of life for Sam and her friends, all they did was train and play:

> I hear now of girls missing training for a sleepover or other event – that was a no, no – we just played. I genuinely can't imagine how life would be without it. There was nothing else that floated my boat at all.

The friends she made then are her friends today:

> Our hang out time was at football – that is where we met and we are still friends now. We are all celebrating our 40ths this year and other friends are joining in and saying about the strong bonds the group of us have. We tell them that is because we have been through a lot of things over the years – done a lot together. It has been kind of nice from that point of view.

However, this way of life ended abruptly in 2012 when Sam suffered a severe knee injury during a game. She recalls that she had not been in the starting team for a few weeks and was surprised by the call-up and thinks that may have meant she was not as well prepared as she would usually be. She said that she instantly knew how serious it was and after the initial shock was thinking, 'right that's me done'. She felt there was no way at 28 she could keep her job and carry out the rehabilitation necessary to get back to the standard to play in the Premier League. She had a further seven surgeries on her knee and her surgeon told her that they did not think she would play again. Sam said she had to be realistic and needed to think of the impact on her job and consequences if she was injured again and needed more surgery.

Sam described life before the injury; there was no free time. She would drive to Forfar at 6am to train before work, back to the office in Dundee, work most of the day and then home, something to eat and then back up to training, home shower and that was that. Her job as a Development Officer with the SFA could include evenings and weekends as well – alongside matches – so football consumed everything. Until it didn't, and she was off work for ten weeks, unable to drive, unable to play.

For Sam, the impact of the injury was huge, 'I was like ok, I will have to accept it BUT biggest thing was feeling I had lost the changing room'" Asked what she meant by this, Sam explained:

> At the time playing in the Premier League, trying to hold a job down, training a lot together all the time we had available, mornings and nights, so I saw them more than my family. I did the injury, I couldn't drive, they were all 25 minutes away from me and I was just sitting watching Coronation Street one night and was thinking – is this it? Is this what you do? So, although I was part of the team, I wasn't in

the changing room, I wasn't round the training venue. I was still a little bit in the group chat, but you didn't know what they were talking about, and I felt I was getting left behind.

Sam thinks that her acceptance of the impact of her injury may be in part because her role at the SFA meant she was still heavily involved in football, just not playing, she was not completely cut off from it. She remained friends with the women she had played with but still missed the special camaraderie associated with being part of a team.

Then there was the revelation. Sam had been doing very little exercise on her knee, as she believed it would not be strong enough for impact exercise. In 2019, she was watching the Women's World Cup and in particular the Scotland match against Argentina. Scotland needed to win and were ahead until the last twenty minutes when Argentina staged a comeback and achieved a draw to knock Scotland out of the competition. Sam said, 'After the match I have never had so much built-up energy in my life and I am like "what just happened", we were so close'. Sam explained that the injury to her knee occurred in the same month that Rachel Corsie had injured hers and there was Rachel playing in a World Cup match while Sam was sat on the sofa! So, in that moment she said to her partner, 'I'm off for a run' and he started laughing and I asked him why and he said, 'Your knee will never survive' but I said, 'I'm going'. She got dressed and ran a kilometre in eleven minutes, returning home her partner asked how her knee was and she said, 'It's sore but my brain is healthier'. She then started running every day and thought that this was good as her leg was starting to feel stronger despite the lack of cartilage in her knee. She was still not kicking a ball but that was all about to change.

Carnoustie Women's Rec Story

As part of her job at the SFA, Sam is involved in delivering schemes funded by the Scottish Government's Cashback for Communities' programme and one of these was the School of Football. This uses football to work with girls who may need a bit more support in school. Sam usually manages the scheme as a whole but during Covid she worked with one hub in particular. She noticed one girl who was particularly good but Sam felt that she was not getting much of a challenge from the other players. So, Sam actually played with the group and came to realise that her knee was actually quite strong. Sam explained:

> Any time before that I would never kick a ball but I kicked the ball on a couple of occasions and did a couple of passes and thought 'that's good', and then decided I wanted to go play 5s or something again.

There were already women's recreational teams in Dunfermline, Kinross and Glenrothes and they had invited Sam to come and play with them but it would have involved a 90-minute drive each way and with a busy job and two young children it was not practical. Sam was a member of the Carnoustie Facebook page and so put out a message to ask if any women were interested in a game and organised a night for them to just come along. That first night 45 women turned up.

Not all of the women had been involved in football before. The group in Carnoustie had women who stopped playing in adulthood; a number who said that they had wanted to play at school and did play a little bit but were not allowed to continue as there was no club for them and perhaps surprisingly a lot of women who had never played but loved the idea of it. Sam says that the mix of experience has continued. She said:

I've got a woman who joined us two weeks ago who said, 'I just want to be part of your group because it looks really cool, I've never really played before' and I was like 'Come on in!'

There is another woman who does not play much football but does cartwheels all down the line. It is this mix that Sam wants to maintain as she believes it fosters a culture of women supporting women, and about understanding each other and being able to just co-exist. Sam recalled that she has had women saying, 'I'm really nervous – I'd love to come along but I'm really nervous'. She says to them, 'Let's go for a coffee, go for a walk, I'll meet you there – 'cos getting out the front door is the hardest thing you'll do – once you are in you won't have an issue'. And she has had that, she has had women sitting in their car watching the session maybe sitting in the car for whole session but next time they have got out of the car and watching and then become part of the group. So, while one woman has never kicked a ball before and someone else has played Premier League, the group can play football together and support each other through that.

At the moment the groups train together and then once a month Sam organises 'football festivals' that brings the groups together. At the festivals, Sam keeps an eye out for anyone who is being that bit more 'competitive' in a game. She explained, 'I go round and if Rona's got the ball and someone is coming in hard on her then it's just a wee tap to say, 'Come on'. Sam is determined that this culture and approach will be maintained. She added, 'This is about women who've never had the chance or haven't had the chance again to play football, to keep a safe space for them to do that. It's about building confidence'.

To assist with building confidence in a controlled way, Sam is trialling a new idea at the festivals – using coloured bands. Sam explained how this works. The idea is that before play starts at the festival, a player picks a red, amber or a green band that they tie around their sock. So, as they are running, other players can know that if they have got the ball and they have the red band it is saying 'I am not that confident, leave me alone, give me a bit of space'. If they have an amber band the woman may be saying, 'I might seem confident but I've got my reservations', while green is 'I am confident, so you can tackle me if you want'. The woman picks the band she is comfortable with that day. This means there can still be an element of interaction and contest but within bounds that are comfortable for the woman and enable her to build confidence and to keep it as a safe space for women to play football.

A constant in the history of women's football in Scotland is that just as there are women that want their game to be recreational, there are those who want to take part in competitive football and have 'something to play for'. The women who take part in the Rec groups are no different and so Sam is looking at ways that a competitive element can be introduced for those who want it while maintaining the recreational side.

In the Carnoustie group there are ten or eleven players who are very good, they are older but it is obvious that they have played football before but they are police officers or work in the prison service or are mums so that they cannot commit to play for a team. However, they also would like something more competitive and some have asked whether the festivals could be made more like a tournament. While Sam is clear that the festivals should not change, she is open to creating different opportunities for the women to be competitive.

For example, Sam is proposing to create some kind of monthly league, possibly seven-a-side, so that a team made up of these more experienced women can play a more competitive game across the region. This would also recognise that they may not all be available every week making eleven-a-side more challenging. For the rest of the groups there will still be the monthly festivals to play in. The women can choose what they want to play in, it's up to them and they might feel different next month to the way they feel this month. Or they might watch the other group and think, 'I could do that'.

Sam said that the idea of tackling is an issue for a number of the women and it is not just about confidence but also the chance of injury as there are some who would not be paid if they were off from work. As a result, the games played at the Sunday sessions are evolving and she has introduced 'relaxed football rules'. These are an adaptation of walking football rules so players are only allowed to touch the ball five times before having to pass it; they cannot hit it hard; they have to score inside the box – so there is no shooting from too far or too hard and the ball cannot be above head height. The difference is that players can still run around and get the aerobic benefits while not worrying about a ball in the face or another injury. This makes up the first hour of the session and then the second hour more traditional football rules are used. Sam explained:

> Women are saying that it is really good because they
> get to practise and build up to going to the main one,
> or 'that's a bit too fast for me so I am going back to
> the relaxed one'.

The group is treated like a team and they have an annual awards night but not with awards like 'Player of the Year' – not the traditional stuff. They have 'Kindest Heart of the Year', 'Most Supportive Person'. When Sam first proposed the idea, she described the presentation night and suggested that perhaps the winners should get a £10 Amazon card or something useful like that instead of a medal. A lot of the women said, 'We never got football trophies and we want them' – so that is what they get and they are proudly displayed in living rooms.

One other thing the group does is to look at ways to gather

kit at reasonable or no cost, as they realised that women cannot spend £150 on boots out of the family budget. Sam reckoned that most of the women will be sizes five, six or seven and so the message went out across the whole football club for donations of old boots when kids get new ones. The same with shin guards and other pieces of equipment.

What are the Benefits of Recreational Football for the Women?
If this is how the women spend time at recreational football, the next question has to be, what does it mean to them? Sam's response was that it is so hard to encapsulate it in one sentence, it is better to give examples:

> Many of the women say, 'I couldn't live without it now' and for one woman the sessions are so important to her health that her workplace make sure she is off on a Sunday night so she can come along to football because they find she is so much happier at work.
>
> Another of the women is originally from Aberdeen-shire and reluctantly moved to Carnoustie with her wife. She had come across the group Facebook post and said to Sam, 'I am really nervous, should I come along?', Sam said 'absolutely' and they went for a coffee and Sam told her she would meet her at the session on Sunday to calm her nerves. She did great and she messaged Sam after her second training session saying, 'I'm lying in my bed crying because I feel like a kid again. I was so scared of moving here I didn't want to move here and now I'll never move away from the town or the football club'.
>
> The women who are mums often say, 'I've finally got something that is for me. I can go to the gym which is great but you are on your own – now I have football which is something that's mine'. It is also

great because their kids are playing for the same football club. Sam said it is cute when you see the dad, the mum and two kids all in the same kit or they are borrowing each other's kit.

One of the women, Farrah, participated in a film produced by the SFA for International Women's Day on the theme of the power of football. She was nervous about coming along but Sam supported her and she ended up loving it. She has lost six stone and gained a lot of confidence. Farrah says in the film, 'Football saved my life'.

Sam said that on paper, the women would not connect, they would never come across each other at all. There are women of all different classes, ages, backgrounds, work experiences, family commitments and different approaches to topics including physical appearance such as doing their nails and hair. Sam said that all the women believe that they would never come across each other let alone be friends but they now do nights out and days out so it is not just the football.

There is also a culture of mutual support and sometimes Sam's commitment to problem solving is used here. Sam recalled that within the group some of the women had a hunch that another member might have been experiencing domestic abuse. They tried to talk to her but they could not get her to open up. So, the group held a charity event for a local domestic abuse charity and raised £1000. Sam asked the charity to come along to the event and they came with leaflets and information. The woman took the information and then went and got the support that she needed. As Sam said:

> If we suspect there may be an issue for one of our group, we will try different things to help – in this case we raised money and helped someone.

This has led to Sam hearing her own phrase about one aspect of the importance of football reflected back at her. She said that the Rec is important to the women because at times their lives are crumbling around them and this is a constant support – as Sam explained:

> The women are saying 'I can't be without my changing room' and it makes me happy – it's a different changing room from mine and individual to them but for many of them its life changing.

Sam added that for her it is about the culture and the concept. It is about understanding each of the barriers that these women have faced their whole lives and then looking to break every single one of them down. The minute someone comes to her with a barrier to why she feels she cannot play; Sam starts to think of ways to fix it or find a way around it and get the women playing. It is so much more than a football group; Sam says that it is football that brought them together and its now a big group of women supporting women.

It is also an idea that has grown and grown with 31 groups across Tayside and Fife alone, making it the biggest growth area by a mile. Sam explained that although at the start this group it was not a target area, it is her job to develop girls' and women's football so it was easy to justify working on it initially and then it was built into her work plans. She explained that she was passionate about it and was in the fortunate position to be in a job that could develop it and things are going so well that it is hoped to roll it out across the country. She added that there is a plan to expand the programme to aim it at fifteen to nineteen year olds. This is because there has been a massive drop-out in the leagues, many saying this is because they want to play but cannot commit with all the other demands in their lives. The aim is to find young women football that is played at a level that they can commit to. It is all part of assisting with women's physical and mental health.

Sam regularly posts details about the groups on social media and so is often asked to either speak to new groups or asked to assist with an issue. She said, If someone says 'I am struggling with this', I'll say right I'm coming to help – so a lot of the time I am going out speaking and chatting to them.

She says that she thinks it is an advantage if one of the people involved in leading the group is a woman with some experience in football and therefore lived experience of potential barriers.

Some of the groups are training two or three times a week and what has been nice to see is that Arbroath now have a team in the women's league. That team came from the women's Rec and the same in Blairgowrie and now a team in Dunfermline are about to join the league. They too were women's Rec teams and the women built their confidence and realised that they did want to commit more time to it and to be more competitive.

Asked how she fits it all in, Sam said, 'You've probably guessed that I love it so I find the time. I just love that these women have gotten into or back into football'.

In talking about progress in the women's game, Sam said that she sees the women's football community as a part of the larger football community. It is such a strong community because women have all had to battle for so long – just to get what they want. So, there is a feeling of a shared challenge. She admits that there are days when it can feel like it is not getting anywhere, not making a difference but then if she sits back and looks at how things have changed since she has been involved, she realises that things have moved on.

For example, at times in a meeting the women's and girls' game will top the agenda, and she feels less like the token woman at events due to the number of women at different levels in the SFA. Sam added that a few weeks ago she had been in the UK Parliament with the SFA Chief Executive talking about women's football and growing the game. So just huge changes in fifteen years never mind 40 years. For Sam, women like Shelia Begbie and Anna Signeul, fought the fight that was needed and as the next generation she and others are benefitting from that and they just need to keep working on it.

Sam then gave a short example from her own life. Her four-year-old daughter has only really been aware of Sam and her friends playing football and one Saturday they were driving down a road in Dundee known as the football mile due to the number of football pitches on both sides of the road. Sam said that as they were driving her daughter suddenly shouted, 'Mum!' and I was like 'What?' and she said, 'There are boys playing football over there!' – so it was a surprise and I was like, 'Boys are allowed to play football?' and she was like, 'Well that's weird'. A big change from the five-year-old Sam being stared at for playing football.

Returning to the women's Rec, Sam said it was exciting times as she can remember more and more groups developing. As women see Farrah's video or read stories, they can say, 'I look like that or I used to be like that – or I can see she struggles to play football, so maybe I can go play'.

As the conversation came to an end, Sam was asked what she would say to a woman reading this in the book, who is interested in joining a group. She replied:

> I would encourage them to go for it – just take that step and if you're nervous get in touch with the group leader and just talk about it.

Within the women's Rec game, there is no age limit, there's no weight limit, no ability limit, no disability limit, no limits'. She then added:

It is just really good and I just want everyone to know
how good it is. Women have got so many battles in
society as it is, this is not one you need to have if
you want to play, we will figure it out for you and we
will individualise it as much as we can so women
can play it.

IN THEIR OWN WORDS
Collected by Sam Milne & Karen Fraser

THE FOLLOWING comments were gathered from women
who play in the recreational football team organised by Sam
Milne. These written responses are taken from a questionnaire
completed by the women as part of the work for this book.

The information is presented as statements made under the
four questions asked, where all have been answered. Those
women who provided a name have been identified but there are
three responses that are anonymous.

Questions:

1. Had you been involved in women's football before you
   joined the group?
2. What made you join the recreational football group?
3. What does being part of the group mean to you?
4. Any other comments.

Responses:

Anonymous

- No but was part of the first girls' team in Carnoustie when
  I was at school.
- Played when I was in school and was in need of some form
  of self-care doing something I enjoy. My son started playing

grassroots football last year and being by the pitch watching him and kicking the ball about with him sparked my love of the game again. Not interested in watching football but love to play!

- Safety and a place where there's no judgement, whatever your background, lifestyle or circumstances. I've just recently joined but feel welcome by everyone. I'm quite quiet till I know someone and have gone through a lot the last few years but I can attend and play without pressure to be someone I'm not. It's definitely a form of therapy for me!
- My son loves that I play for the same club as he does and likes that I am trying to get fit again. He would like a match against our women's team!

Anonymous
- Played at youth level.
- Wanted to meet new people, improve fitness and play a sport that I used to love playing.
- So much! It's means much more than just a game of football. It's a space where women support women on and off the field. Personally it's made a huge difference to my mental and physical health.

Anonymous
- Yes.
- Fun and fitness.
- Buckets of fun and banter.
- Literally did not expect to make new friends at my age. Didn't think I had room in my life for any more lovely people. Now I would have a massive gap in my life if they weren't there. I love how everyone is sooooo different and when you put all the individual parts together you somehow stumble on a winning formula. It's accidental magic.

Debbie

- No.
- Looking for a hobby and to make new friends.
- Honestly, everything. I have played team sports all my life, but never have I come across such a lovely, welcoming, supportive group of women. They have become real friends and I look forward to Sunday nights more than I ever thought was possible.

Farah

- Two years.
- I wanted to get fit and healthy and get back to playing football.
- It's completely changed my life. I've lost 6.5 stone in weight. I have put my Type 2 diabetes into remission. I've built a massive support network of incredible women who are my biggest champion. They always have my back, have motivated, empowered and inspired me to keep going. I owe them this new body and new life.
- If you are thinking about recreational football, give it a go you've got nothing to lose!

Kerry

- No.
- A friend recommended it.
- It means everything. Life wouldn't be the same without this every Sunday.

Laura

- No.
- To play football and have fun.
- It's been great, the girls are all amazing and we have the best laugh. It's almost like therapy for some of us and time away from kids, work and the stresses of life.

- I highly recommend joining a women's rec team, it's done a lot for me and the girls have supported me through a tough diagnosis even when I've not been able to attend they have reached out to me. We are like a family!

Paula
- No.
- Enjoyed playing football when I was younger and wanted to get back into playing and to help my fitness.
- Everyone is on their own journey but come together to have fun through the enjoyment of football.
- Best decision I made in 2023.

Rhona
- No.
- My work colleague suggested I come and try.
- The girls are so encouraging and supportive. I now have a new network of friends and contacts.
- I love being part of this team. I came into the sport very late in life, wish I had done it sooner. I am so happy to have something for me now after spending last 18 years raising a family.

Sarah
- Never.
- My friend sang its praises until I relented and came along!
- The camaraderie, fun and support has been amazing. We are all firm friends and meet up regularly outside of football now.
- It really helped my mental health during a stressful time in my life. I have dealt with my family's addictions, deaths and all kinda of awful events and I honestly couldn't have got through it without both the physical and mental release of activity every week and the amazing support of Sam and the rest of our team.

Siobhan

- Yes, when I was a teenager, but not as an adult.
- A team local to me started up and a friend let me know and asked if I wanted to attend.
- It means having a sense of belonging and being accepted for who you are. Playing football with the girls is amazing because you meet people from all walks of life and get the chance to make friends with people you otherwise wouldn't have spoken to. Being part of the group is knowing that there's always someone there when you need them. It's encouragement to get involved even if you've never played football before.
- The girls I play with are some of the most supportive people I've ever met. I'm so proud of each and every one of them. I'm especially grateful to have met Sam. Not only has she facilitated the whole group and got us to where we are today, she had been such a supportive person in my life and has been there for me both in and out of football. I'm so thankful for her and all of the wonderful women I've met through this team.

Scotty

- Yes, but years before! I had to stop playing due to injury, and there was never an opportunity to continue playing at a rec level with other women – only with the guys. I didn't mind playing 5s with the guys but it was never the same.
- My friend from uni ask me to come along and the rest is history! I'm not sure if I would have attended as I had been so used to playing in a team environment, where there was always completion to play/start. My only regret is that I didn't start sooner!
- Words can't capture the profound significance this group holds for me. It's more than just a team of girls; it's a bond, a sanctuary where I find solace. Every moment spent playing

football with them, that precious hour and a half each week, is an escape. It's a reprieve from the challenges of my week, a chance to shed the weight of worries, and simply be myself. In the embrace of the game, I am accepted unconditionally. This group is more than teammates; they are my support network, my confidantes, true friends. Within the lines of the field, I'm not alone. It's a place where judgments fade away, and genuine connections flourish. Playing football with these incredible women has given me a haven, a cherished something to look forward to each week. It's not just a game; it's a lifeline, a source of joy and camaraderie. The unity we share transcends the boundaries of the field, creating memories and forging a bond that extends far beyond our playing time. This group has become my anchor, grounding me in moments of uncertainty. I would do anything for these girls because, in them, I've found more than teammates – I've found a family, a treasure trove of support, laughter and unwavering acceptance. I love Sundays and eagerly anticipate each week with a heart full of gratitude.

Vicki

- No.
- Covid restrictions at first...I was looking to exercise outdoors and had always enjoyed kicking a ball around so I joined.
- Being part of the woman's rec is everything, from joining just to get fresh air and exercise to releasing how important being with the girls and having that bond on the pitch and off, has such an impact on a lot of things. For me, it's not only helped with my fitness but my confidence on and off the pitch has grown. I don't think I can attribute that to anything else except the woman's rec football – I love it!

INCHES

Julie McNeill

These games are won
and lost in inches,
in scuffs and snatches,
trips and pullbacks.
They are tipped by balance.

Plant your feet now
Raise your heads
and see what you have done
with games lost
and games won.

Our expectations grow
because you made it so.

Tonight, wide-eyed
my daughter watched you play
she dreams of being you, one day.
Her jacket's
in the wash again,
boggin' from masquerading
as a goalpost in the mud.

She's ditched the school skirt
for a Scotland strip
and plasters her walls
with posters of you.

She doesn't measure
her team in inches.
The mud-splats
and missed shots
bring her back to the centre spot
Where she will rise and fall
and rise again.

TYNECASTLE 23 OCTOBER 2020

David McVey

Four silent stands. No bellows or roars.
No octave-higher 'Let's go Scotland, let's go!'
We're unheard, unvoiced, watching telly.
The anthems echo thinly, choirless, and fade.

Talk to your plants, it's said, they'll flourish.
But will the Flower of Scotland blossom
without vocal willing or encouragement?
Or will the seeds shirk the silence, dormant?

The 'little white rose of Scotland' takes root,
pushes into the light, grows stronger.
'Sharp and sweet', it 'breaks the heart' yet
outblooms the brave red poppy of Albania.

90 minutes on, the white rose looms above
the poppy, which struggles in Scotland's
        sour soil.
Our flower is tall and proud and strong,
but how we long to nurture it with our voices.

In Their Own Words
Collected by Karen Fraser

IN THIS BOOK, I have written a short essay about the interviews I undertake with women who have played football between 1960 and now. One of the great delights of undertaking these interviews is hearing about both the women's love of the game and the barriers they faced in order to play the game. Below are some extracts from interviews with the women describing these things in their own words.

Sub-standard Facilities and Lack of Officials

Facilities then were terrible, more like a gardener's shed thing. There were a couple of changing rooms, a few chairs lying about, cramped facilities and lucky if any showers and if there were, they were grotty. Other clubs were all much of a muchness, all just playing on the council parks with normal council facilities. (Jane)

So, you would have things hanging off the handles of a lawnmower or some different kind of a machine and it was really pretty awful actually particularly in terms of training, especially if it was cold or it had been raining because you couldn't have a shower or anything, it was really pretty horrific. (Sheila)

The changing room was the bottom flat in the block which was a women's refuge. We would change in the living room and walk up to training ground. With other teams, you would turn up at there would be no facilities, so you would change in the back of a car, change on the bus, there were no toilets and no showers. (Kate)

If you forgot to book the pitch you had to take what you were given. Some of the places were no more than a field, full of puddles, you couldn't run properly and the ball would keep getting stuck. (Marion)

We played on blaes for so long 'cos no one else would take it, so the women got it. It was luxury to play on grass. (Kate)

Some [pitches] were worse than others, near Ravenscraig it was an ashen pitch and gravelly and I had to have a penicillin injection because I had taken all the skin off my legs – so a few bad ones. (Susan)

Playing matches, we just booked the pitch if it was a home game and that was one of my responsibilities. It would just be a local pitch in East Kilbride, no changing facilities – it was just public parks, had to watch out for broken glass, dog shit, they weren't always in the best condition. (Fiona)

We used to train on muddy grass fields with no goals, use our jackets for goals and probably wouldn't even have cones at the time and five footballs between us. (Emma)

We had some good referees and some terrible ones and sometimes no referees at all. So, the teams would find people but that often ended up in a barney, a fight would start and then everyone would go back playing. (Magi)

Making Time to Play in Busy Lives, as in Scotland at the Time, Football Could Not be the 'Career'

Football was the priority and other things fitted in around it – so I was lucky enough to be able to change my hours at work to fit the football 7am–3pm and then at 3pm getting a bus to the Commonwealth Pool to train and that was Monday through to Friday. Sometimes on a Saturday I would train as well and then game on a Sunday– that was my life and I fitted other things in between it. (Jane)

I was a residential worker – early, late, night shifts – if late go to gym in morning, if early then could go to training. To get every Sunday off I did a double shift on a Saturday swapping with one of the guys I knew who did a double shift on a Sunday. (Amy)

I was in control of my own time working 9–5. I was offered to do shifts when I was 22/23 but said no because it wouldn't fit in with the football...I got to training, got to games because I was a day shift. (Maureen)

It Was the Love of the Game That Motivated and Rewarded the Women

I think what happened the second night was, I was given a holdall, a football holdall. It was black and I can still smell it, that black plastic. It had green lettering saying Monklands LFC and oh my God that was just like fantastic. (Magi)

I just loved it – I loved playing. (Maureen)

Football gave me everything, it's my life, I have gone through a hard time in my life and football has got me through it. Opportunities that I will be forever grateful for...given me confidence, lets me come out of my comfort zone, football changes your life and made me the person I am today. (Emma)

Then when it happened it was like a dream come true – to pull on a strip and be part of a team – I remember standing there and looking at myself and thinking this is brilliant. (Chris).

There is nothing like being on the pitch, not thinking about anything else in life for 90 minutes. There would be a point in time when you could see the team needed something and you could work out what that was and do it. I got a buzz out of that – days off go up the park with a bag of balls and practise free kicks and then when you got one in the game you could tell that was because of the practice. Doing things on a pitch that you thought about doing and then can do – 'I'm going to put that in the top corner' and then you do, that is a great sense of achievement. (Pauline)

NOTES:

Marion Barclay was involved in the 1970s and early 1980s. She played in Scotland at elite club level and for the Scottish Women's National Team and continued to play when she moved to Canada.

Sheila Begbie was involved from the 1970s to mid-2010s She played at club level, captained the Scottish Women's National Team and worked for both Sportscotland and the SFA in development roles.

Kate Cooper has been involved from the 1980s to date. She played at elite club level and was a volunteer committee member for SWF. She is currently a club coach for SWFL club.

Fiona Edwards was involved in the 1980s and 1990s. She played at semi-serious club level. She also qualified as a referee and was Treasurer of the SWFA.

Magi Hamilton was involved from the 1970s to 1990s. She played at semi-serious club level. She also coached youth football and was Chair of the SWFA in early 1990s.

Pauline Harvey was involved from the 1990s to 2019. She played at elite and semi-serious level clubs.

Chris Henderson was involved in the 1980s. She played at elite club level.

Emma Hunter has been involved from the 1980s to date. She played at elite club level and age group Scottish Women's National Team. She is currently co-coach of SWPL club.

Jane Legget was involved in the 1970s and 1980s. She played at elite level club and for Scottish Women's National Team. She moved to England and also played there.

Amy McDonald was involved from 1990s to 2023. She played at elite club level and with the Scottish Women's National Team. She qualified as a coach and was head coach for a club in the SWPL.

Maureen Simms was involved from the 1990s to 2010s. She played at elite club level.

Susan Williams was involved from the mid-1970s through to early 1990s. She played at semi-serious club level.

DEAR FOOTBALL COACH

Morag Anderson

the trials flyer pinned
to the pock-marked board
beside the inter-school league scores

asks for good ball control.
I use feet, legs, head, and chest
with a clean first touch.

I manage the ball close,
maintain possession
with easy aggression.

I send the ball
to the desired destination
with powerful precision.

I am fluid with long strides,
hold a low centre of gravity
if occasion demands.

I assess the risk-reward,
minimise energy spend.
Play smart, not hard.

I create opportunity
then attack. Force
opponents to backtrack.

I endure stress, fatigue,
and all things adverse.
I move fast in a small space

to win, keep, protect the ball;
perform under pressure
with composure.

I accept defeat without regret.
So tell me why
'Girls Need Not Apply'?

Pioneers & Heroines

In this section you will find poems and short essays about the women and events that have shaped women's football in Scotland across the years.

THE CROWDS' LOVE SONG

Abiy Orr

Kick it for us,
Those never asked to join the dance,
Who find no friends, who get no chance:
Kick it for us.

Kick it for us,
The unvoiced and the voiceless ones,
The ones whose moment never comes:
Kick it for us.

Kick it for us,
The slow, the ill, the crushed, the lame;
Frightened too far or raised too tame:
Kick it for us.

Kick it for us,
Stoking our fire with every stride –
You bring us strength, you give us pride:
Kick it for us.

Kick it for us
And take us flying up the wing,
Fill us with hope and hear us sing,
Kick it for us.

Kick it for us
And never mind the final score.
We're here with you, we ask no more:
Kick it for us.

IT'S HER

Linda Jackson

Clydebank hardship. Emotional mayhem
a life torn and thrown in the winds of neglect.
Tall and strong,
fast and furious, she kicked the ball far and wide
into the park   by the river   around the school,
wherever...
She kicked the ball high, offside,
off kilter with rage in every stride she took.
Heidie kicks behind the dinner school
aw the boys tackled her hard
but she easy got past them
then past that life to move on, shoot and turn
in a tide of learning.
Central Park, New York – taking a chance,
nineteen and football with the street boys
brought new lessons till the coach from Texas
pushed the scholarship,
put wings in her boots
panic to the touchline.
Wise coach who inspired, controlled the fire
Focus your rage, channel the sea of power, score!
Goal mouth blootered, she turns away quiet
stadium erupts, heart settles down knowing
who she is.
Clydebank to Carolina, Carolina to Milan
Italy for years, a professional woman footballer
Player now coach, passing it on,
the marking, the tackling, the sea of energy when she ran

It's her, that lassie fae Clydebank, ye know the wan.

ELSIE – IN HER AIN WURDS
Elsie Cook

Stewarton Thistle Ladies Football Club

Ma real love affair (obsession) with playing the actual game itsel began in 1961 wae the formation of Stewarton Thistle Ladies Football Club. Ma mither came hame fae church this Sunday and says tae me:

> You ken a bit aboot fitba hen, well, the Provost, Walter Syme, has asked me tae get the netball lassies thegither tae play a fitba match against his ladies works' team. It's a wummin's team!

'A wummin's team?' I repeated, shriekin' wae laughter!'
'Wummin don't play fitba!'

'Jist haud yer wheesht Elsie! Well', continued ma mither, 'these wummin dae and it's tae raise funds for Charity, for the Freedom From Hunger Campaign.'

I knew aboot these Ethiopian weans dyin wae starvation, it was aw ower the television news. Oor minister even spoke aboot it fae the pulpit. So, I agreed tae sound ma pals oot aboot 'playing' fitba. So, Stewarton Thistle LFC came into being on 1 May 1961. Netball coach, mum, mustered the netball players thegither and I talked ma fitba pals intae makin up the numbers. The Provost's East Kilbride factory were lookin' for opposition and we were it.

Ma mither, aye wan for a fundraisin challenge, of course, had said, aye. Nothin was ever too much bother for ma mither and her twa sisters, Nancy and Helen, so between them and the netball lassies the idea of kickin a baw instead o catchin it was done and dusted. This was unheard of, wummin playing football! Wummin in these days, were hoosewives and full-time mothers, end of. Wummin were only on this earth tae care for their men. Not many wummin went out to work especially if they had children and a husband to care for. Wummin did not wear the 'troosers', literally!

In the mid-fifties, early sixties, wummin spent most of their time, in the kitchen and the scullery. Remember, nae washing machines, microwaves, hoovers, fridges, disposable nappies and takeaways in thae days. Wummin were aye busy! It went withoot sayin. It was expected. Yet here we were, invited, by the most famous and respected man in the toun, the Provost, to play a charity football match against his wummin's team, Holyrood Bumbees!

They were an experienced team so we started training right away, the game was in two weeks' time.

We were aw so excited! Mum had said, 'Elsie, you and yer pals ken the gemme inside oot wae followin' Killie, we really need you three.'

So, we had seven netball players, masel and ma pals fae Rugby Park and that was us – Stewarton Thistle LFC absolutely ready tae take oan anyone. Excitin days, for me and pals, Liz and Madge, Killie faithfuls, hame or away. We'd never really kicked a baw and were relatively new to the game but we knew the rules, that, was a start. A first get together and trainin session was organised. Ma uncle, Wull Fleming, and a couple of his mates, twa weel kent Stewarton characters, Tiger Gorrie and Wullie Gillespie, took the trainin. They were a riot of both laughter and genuine endeavour and we were aw told the rules, what positions we'd be playin and the role that these positions had tae play in the gemme. Surprise, oor goalie was tae be Nessie, Jimmy Broon, the Killie goalie's wife. We couldnae lose, could we?

So, Stewarton Thistle LFC were up and ready tae roll, but, heck, it turned oot that Nessie wisnae gonnae be available, she had only jist found oot that she was pregnant, so, we were still a coupla players short of a full team. Now here comes my first inspiration. The incredibly talented Kilmarnock lassie, fae Riccarton, Susan Ferries. The week before the proposed match, the boys on the supporter's bus were laughin at the idea of us lassies being in a fitba team. They were good natured boys, oor mates. We were aw fitba daft, and shared an awful lot of good times wae Killie, oor team.

Before the gemme at Rugby Park oan a Setterday, Matt, the young groundsman, wid produce a baw and we'd have a wee gemme on the trainin pitch afore the real gemme kicked aff. We lived and breathed fitba! We were as one. Well, the mair the boys thocht aboot it, the mair they liked the idea of us lassies formin a fitba team. Even the aulder guys oan oor supporters bus were behind the idea. Eggin us oan. They thocht it might just be possible, a one off, for a laugh.

An older guy piped up:

> Elsie there's a lassie doon the road fae me in Riccarton, oh my, can she kick a baw, she's better than aw the men, runs rings roon them, wae that baw never far fae her foot. Great control skills, powerfa heider o a baw and whit a shot she has! She leas' us aw staunin' gaping, oor mooths hingin' open in awe. My goad ye daurna try and tackle her or she'll even pit the boot in! Aye, she's a hardy yin. She's tean fae naebody! Ask onybody! You boys ken whit she's capable o!

says he, lookin' aroon the bus!

> You should get her. Her name's Susan Ferries, fae Jeffrey Street in Riccarton! I'll ask her if she'd like a gemme for ye. Gie me the match details! I'm tellin' ye, she maks fools o the men wae her close control and mazy runs and...she is tough! Disnae staun ony nonsense! Naebody messes wae Susie!

So, he got in touch wae Susie, and wonder of wonders, she agreed tae take part!

Noo aw we needed was a baw, a strip and boots. Baw and strips borrowed fae Jock Roy's men's team, also called Stewarton Thistle. The word went roon the toun that the new lassies team were lukin for boots. So funny...as boots of aw sorts, even boots wae the wooden hammer in studs, turned up at Riverside Road! Boots of all conditions and sizes arrived at oor hoose. Then the lassies came along, found a pair nearest tae their size, tried them on, took them hame and proudly polished them up wae a thing ca'd 'Dubbin', we need tae look smart!

The baw, the auld leather lace up baw wae a bladder. Dae yooz hae mind, the stitchin oan the baw wid burst noo and again and the pink bladder wid bubble oot and ye'd poke it back in and cairry oan!

I made posters advertisin the gemme. These posters went up in every shop windae aroon the toun and aw the talk fae the tounsfolk was aboot this big match, a 'wummin's gemme'. Aye ye could hear folk mutter incredulously, but, in fact, everyone was up for it. In Stewarton back then, everybody kent everybody in the toun. So, it was, by poster and word of mooth, an expectant, yet 'm sure, dubious, crowd of ower 500 was expected tae turn up at Strandhead Park, Stewarton, on 1 May 1961 tae watch twenty twa daft lassies kick a baw aboot! We scrambled aboot for twa weeks gettin equipment thegither. Ma uncle, Wull, ran the Churches League team and his mates, Willie and Tiger, soon knocked us intae shape.

Efter a coupla sessions they gave us our positions. I was proud to be made centre hauf and captain. I was tae be Stewarton's Frank Beattie! Only similarity tae Frank, of course, was the captaincy! Me! Captain! Wow! We were mair excited as the days went by. It was aw we talked aboot.

The hale toun was so up for this. Havin read the posters in the shops and adverts in oor local paper, the *Kilmarnock Standard* well, it was lukin guid. It was a novelty. Aye, some folk laughed. Stewarton folk were honest tae the point of being 'blunt'. Some derided us, weemin as well as men: 'Weemin wantin' tae play fitba Bella, for Goads' sake whit next?' ye could hear them gossipin' in the street and laughin' ower the back doors as they hung their washin' oot...but some were encouragin' too, it was a stert.

The Provost organised the pitch and referee and as the proceeds were for the 'Freedom from Hunger Campaign', we were allowed to use Strandhead, the cooncil park, and changin facilities. The church's Women's Guild baked and were going tae lay on a post-match tea for us. It was aw lookin' guid! The big day arrived, match day! Electric atmosphere inside the changin rooms. Nae word fae Susan Ferries but I was assured she'd be there.

Nae aunt Helen: 'Where's aunt Helen mum?' says I.

'Och! Shoosh! She's found oot she's pregnant again!' was mum's reply, 'But Jessie Steele's here!'

Disaster averted! Still a player short, naebody had heard a cheep fae Susan Ferries.

The Holyrood Bumbees arrived in style in a private bus. We welcomed them and showed them tae their 'away' dressin' room while we were individually introduced to their boss, oor toun Provost, Mr Walter Syme. The excitement was risin. The strips hangin in suspense on their respective pegs! I can still see, smell and sense that dressin room even 60 years later. The atmosphere was thick and tangible wae that strong smell of Dubbin and Sloane's Horse Rub. I always hae mind o the magic of Sloane's Rub, and the smell, a real fitba smell, pervadin the air. Half an hour tae kick off: the townsfolk were arrivin noo and noisily findin a spot by the railings aroon Strandhead Park. There was such guid humour in the atmosphere. Yet, here we were, still a player short and still nae sign of oor would be 'star' player, Susan Ferries.

Lacin up ma, twa sizes, too big 'Pele' boots, aye, they had Pele's signature oan the side. Stuffin the taes wae newspaper. Wae an auld folded up *Sunday Post* doon the front o ma shins for protection, I'm thinkin, we're still wan player short. I'm feelin the tension gettin tae me.

Excitedly hangin aboot the clubhouse, heart racin, waitin for Susan Ferries tae arrive. Everyone noisily gigglin and chatterin awa wae nerves. Then a loud cry went up:

'Elsie! Here's Susan..!'

Anither shout went up:

'Aye! There she is Elsie! There's Susie!'

Susan came fae a fitba family, her faither, Bill, had been a grand player wae the famous top junior team, Auchinleck Talbot in his day! I leapt tae ma feet and ran oot the clubhoose, studs clatterin aff the flair.

I couldnae see onybody that looked like a fitba player! Oh my!

Ye could've knocked me doon wae a feather! Noo, seriously, I couldnae see onybody fittin the description I'd been given o Susan Ferries, I could only see, a young, curly, blonde comin through the park gates, couldnae be her, could it? Could it really be this braw, curly-heided lassie, dressed in the style o the time? A roon necked, white, sleeveless, print frock, covered in huge red roses, complete wae starched, sticky oot petticoats and high heels. She swaggered gallusly, confidently, through the Strandhead Park gates, swingin a broon leather shoppin bag, wae new boots that she'd jist bought for the gemme, fae a secondhaun' shop, Cheapside Bargains in Bank Street, Kilmarnock. That was Susan! These same boots that she wore every gemme throughout her twelve-year career wae Stewarton Thistle are now, deservedly, in pride of place alongside her Scotland cap, in the SFA Football Museum.

'YES!'

I actually shouted it oot. It had tae be Susan...so it was, the one and only, Susan Ferries.

'Sorry am late, a got aff at the wrang bus stoap', says she. My young, fit, cousin, Moira, had agreed tae make up the numbers, if required, but there we were, a full team, and we're aw set tae kick aff. Inside the changin rooms, the tension was mountin. We were so excited, nervous, breathless and giggly pullin on oor strips, shorts and boots for the first time, was a huge occasion. Anticipation growin.

The Bumbees were already stripped, rarin tae go. We still had nae goalkeeper! Oor goalie was to be Nessie Brown, but Nessie hadnae turned up yet!

Then ma auntie Nancy, oor left back, whispered, 'Elsie, wheesht, yer mither already telt ye, Nessie cannae play, and neither can auntie Helen, they're baith pregnant!'

'I'd forgotten! Uncle Wull says, 'Anne Thomson in goals.'

Oor very first match! Wae 30 meenits tae kick aff! Aw, honestly, in aw the hype, I'd forgotten! So, twa young netball players switched position. Ann Thomson in goals. Ebeth Paton gaun tae left-back.

George Anderson, the referee, came in and introduced himself tae baith teams, checked the studs and we all proudly marched oot thegither, in twa lines behin' him.

George was actually defyin the SFA ban against aidin' wummin's football. This, a ban we still actually knew nothing' aboot and we only learned later, that he could've been censored, disciplined for agreein' to assist us. George wisnae aware o any ban or the fact he was takin' a chance.

Provost Syme made a short speech to baith teams and the crowd, explainin that this was a charity match, funds in aid of the dreadful famine in Ethiopia.

'Right ladies...go on oot there and enjoy yersels!'

Oh! We wid, I thocht. This was oor big day, and amidst cheers fae the crowd, which included ma pals, the boys fae the scheme, Provost Syme announced baith teams tae an expectant audience. Referee, George, spoke tae us: 'Nae nonsense lassies, watch yer language!'

Oor language George? This was a serious business and the referee proodly led baith teams ontae the pitch. Ma stomach was churnin. Ma mooth wis dry wae excitement. Ma legs shoogly, like jelly! I was captain and was so up for it.

We marched ontae the field like pros. We captains shook hauns. The coin tossed, I elected tae shoot doonhill, intae the bottom goals, first hauf. Some of the Killie players had come along to cheer us on. Eric Murray, Bobby Ferguson and Josie Mason. How guid o them. Lots of shoutin' and encouragement fae the sidelines as we kicked aff. Loud instructions shouted fae oor coaches, Uncle Wull, Tiger and Willie, keepin' us right, reverberated richt aroon the park.

The team lined up thus:

> Ann Thomson in goals, auntie Nancy Fleming, right-back, Ebeth Paton left-back, ma mither, Betty Bennett, right-hauf, masel, Elsie Bennett, centre-hauf, Anna Rafferty left-hauf, Elaine Russell ootside-right, head-mistress, Jessie Steel, inside-right, Susan Ferries centre-forward, wae ma pal, Madge McKie, inside-left and ma ither pal, Liz Lochhead (Hurlford Utd footballer, Jim Lochhead's sister), on the left wing.

Within meenits, we were shown jist whit Susie Ferries could dae wae a baw at her feet. Her incredible close ball control, strong, unstoppable shot! Well, we were up three goals within the first twenty minutes, wae ma mither screamin' instructions at us aw tae, 'Nae footerin' lassies jist gie the baw tae Susie!' At hauf time wae the score being 5–0, Susie had scored all five goals.

The game was really nothin' tae get excited aboot, we lassies didnae really offer much in the way of entertainment but Susan, well, Susan was in a class of her own. Susan *was* the entertainment. She ran the entire show wae the crowd, men and weemin, enthusiastically shoutin' her on. She'd pick the baw up in midfield, mazy run forward, easily beatin', one, two, three defenders and blooterin' it intae the roof o the net. Great wae wee cheeky goals as well, sidesteppin' the Bumbee keeper, slidin' it hame, and a powerful heider o a baw. Susan was fearless. Susan had it aw. She controlled that entire match. Dribbled that baw effortlessly. Ten meenits intae the gemme, even at 2–0, I could hear the crowd encouraging her, to score more. Tae this day I can still hear ma mither enthusiastically screamin', 'Gie the baw tae Susie!' any time we were oan the baw. The crowd were lovin' every second o Susie oan that baw.

So, we'd done oor job. We'd run oor legs aff. We had passed tae Susan and we had won oor very first gemme 7–0! Susie had scored all seven goals. Whit a gemme, whit an introduction, tae actually, playin' fitba. We were on a high and wanted mair. I wisnae gonnae let this be a wan off. We were in awe of Susie. She was the catalyst, the inspiration for me to keep pushin' the wummin's gemme tae prove that weemin could and should be encouraged tae play fitba. I had found a purpose in ma life. The local crowd were ecstatic and whits mair, they were complimentary. As I said, I could hear the crowd's comments fae the sidelines:

'Wid ye luk at that for a shot.'

'Whit a goal, we've no seen mony better goals scored at Strandhead Park.'

This fae an auld Stewarton worthy, Jock Porter, a guid striker in his day, tae his brither, Andra Porter, who, incidentally, was a crackin' goalkeeper of some merit. These accolades were well appreciated, especially by masel and ma Killie fitba pals.

Oor backroom boys, uncle Wull, Tiger and Willie were ower the moon. I could see the pride in their e'en as they excitedly egged us oan fae the sideline. We'd been ridiculed afore the match wae the oft repeated 'Weemin cannae play fitba, it's a man's gemme.'

Well we were vindicated, Susie was oor hero and lauded aff the park by fans and players alike. Susie was a wan aff wummin, a fitba superstar, successfully challengin' the realms of men.

I noo took oan the mammoth but rewardin' task of keepin' the team thegither, wae the sole purpose of 'showcasin' Susan Ferries. Immediately efter that first match, we're aw bletherin an talkin aboot carryin'oan playin, if we could find opposition, when I was telt a wee boy, a wee seven-year auld boy was luckin for me, askin for a gemme.

Somebody pointed me oot as the manager. The wee guy wae a short back and sides, heavy plastic baw under his airm, spots me. Strides up tae me.

'Haw Mrs.'

Mrs? I was fourteen!

This was a maist memorable date. No jist because of it bein' a first wummin's fitba match played in Stewarton, or of Susan Ferries's prowess wae a baw, naw this was anither reason tae remember the date. On 1 May 1961, I was approached on the immaculate puttin' green, adjacent tae the fitba park, by a superstar tae be. I looked the wee 'boy' up and doon and telt him, 'Och! Sorry son it's a lassies' team, ye cannae play in a lassies team', to which he replied indignantly, 'But a am a lassie!' On that, I realised 'he' was in fact a 'she'.

'Well, you come back in a coupla years' time and we'll see! Two years! Ok?' says I.

Well, this wis in fact a wee seven-year-auld, innocent, shiny faced, Rose Reilly. Rose can be seen keekin in oan the left-hand side of oor very first team photo and she did, true tae her word, come back and play for Stewarton Thistle LFC exactly twa years later. Age nine! Rose turned up at Strandhead Park in 1963 and played her very first gemme for Stewarton Thistle LFC v Johnstone Red Rockets. I wisnae tae ken then, just how this wee lassie wid go oan tae achieve great things. This wee 'boy' of course, none ither than the Rose Reilly who wid achieve fame at hame and mair especially, star abroad in Italy's Serie A.

As a young lassie in a male-orientated Scotland, we lassies, growin' up, were constantly treated as second-class citizens. Restricted by oor gender, as second best in maist things. Yet, here I was, in awe of Susan's ability and there and then, I decided, this was to be ma crusade. I'd support, promote and advertise the fact that fitba wisnae the sole domain of men. How dare they try and ban us. Ma mission was to be a journey fu o purpose. Weemin and young lassies could and should participate in the greatest gemme on earth, as Pele ca'd it, 'The Beautiful Game'. And so it was. And so it began: 1 May 1961, Strandhead Park, Stewarton.

Picture of Stewarton Thistle LFC on
the day they were formed, 1 May 1961.
Front row left is Susan Ferries; right is Elsie Cook.
The young girl on the far left looking at the camera is
seven-year-old Rose Reilly. [*Elsie Cook, personal archive.*]

ELSIE COOK

Karen Fraser

ACROSS THE HISTORY of women's football in Scotland there have been events or people who have moved the progression of the game forward significantly. Elsie Cook is one of the people who drove women's football forward in the 1960s and first half of the 1970s through her work to assist in setting up a fledgling infrastructure and involvement in several notable events. This work further strengthened the foundations of the women's football in Scotland we enjoy today.

In 1961, Betty Bennett worked at Holyrood Knitwear where the managing director, Walter Syme, was also Lord Provost of Kilmarnock. The factory had a women's football team called the Holyrood Bumbees – no, not a spelling mistake, that was their name! The Lord Provost wanted to raise money for charity and thought a women's football match would be a good way to do this. He asked Betty to get together a group of women who could play against the established team. She turned to her daughter, who was a fan of men's football for assistance. Elsie's involvement changed the course of her life and accelerated the development of Scottish women's football.

Elise set about forming a team from members of her netball team, relatives and one or two women who she knew played football.

The team, known as Stewarton Thistle, beat the established Holyrood Bumbees team and decided to remain together as a team. Elsie worked hard to find other players and to find other teams to play against. In a time before social media and easy access to phones, this was not easy and was initially achieved through word of mouth. A team you played against knew of another team, contact was made, often by letter, and games arranged. You would hear about other women players who have been spotted having a kick-about with the lads at work or who had mentioned they were interested in playing and sometimes younger girls who hung around the team hoping to get a game.

Playing a game was itself a major feat of organisation. As women's football was still restricted, the spaces to play included local parks and council pitches. With no storage available all equipment had to be carried to the pitch – often on the bus – and nets put up and lines painted as necessary. For some of the women getting to a game could mean two or more buses – if they were running – as games at to be played on a Sunday when men's teams were not using the pitches.

It was Elsie's enthusiasm, encouragement and sheer stubbornness that saw Stewarton Thistle become one of the best of the well-known teams at the time. Within the limited writing on women's football in Scotland in the 1960s and early 1970s, there were only a handful of teams regularly mentioned. This is because those doing the writing only had a small number of known women players to speak to in Scotland, with Elsie being one of them. Elsie spoke to these authors about the teams she was aware of, and the number reported remained at twelve for a long time. More recently, it has become clear that there were more than 80 teams playing across Scotland at this time but with no easy means of communication or raising awareness, they played in their own geographical area, largely unaware of other teams or too far apart to play each other on a regular basis.

But back to Elsie and Stewarton Thistle, the Scottish Cup, the formation of a national league and the first international match. While some of the women were content to play the occasional game, many others wanted to have the chance to have 'something to play for'. In 1968, Elsie and Stewarton Thistle had been part of the group of ten teams that formed an unofficial league. In 1970, Elsie was interviewed by a newspaper and when asked how the paper could support women's football, Elsie asked them to donate a cup. The cup was first played for by a group of invited teams (the ones Elsie had regular contact with at the time) across 1970/71. On 18 April 1971, Stewarton Thistle, beat the Aberdeen Prima Donnas to become the first-ever winners of the Scottish Cup.

Teams from this group were also taking part in competitions organised by those interested in women's football in England. These included the Butlin's Cup, the Deal International Tournament. Involvement in the inaugural Mitre Cup, organised by the English Women's Football Association (WFA) was to prove extremely important for Elsie, Stewarton Thistle and women's football in Scotland.

Unlike the Butlin's Cup competition which was designed to end in an England vs Scotland final, the Mitre Cup was organised in a traditional format with teams being drawn to play in ties to progress through the competition. Stewarton Thistle beat several English teams on their way to the final and did so in a convincing manner. Indeed, their progression through the tournament was so strong that it may have led to an attempt to ensure that on the first time of awarding it, the cup stayed in England. The contention is that the Southampton team that Stewarton were due to meet was replaced with a league select eleven for the final. There is no official confirmation of this although Elise received a phone call to inform her and the English teams in the third place play off withdrew in protest. Asked about it at the time, Elsie, the Stewarton captain said, 'I am not surprised, they couldn't allow a Scottish club to lift their first FA Cup – no way'.

Despite the loss, the experience made Elsie even more determined to claim a place for the women's game in the Scottish football community. In 1972, she and others involved in teams in the unofficial league, invited all thirteen teams then participating to attend a meeting in Edinburgh. Six teams attended and, on 17 September 1972, they formed the Scottish Women's Football Association (SWFA). For those involved, the point of the SWFA was to demonstrate the strength of interest in women's football and the desire to promote it further. At the meeting, Elsie was appointed as the first SWFA secretary and set about organising not only the first official women's football league comprising twelve teams but the first official women's international between Scotland and England.

The match was held on 18 November 1972 at Ravenscraig Park, in Greenock, with England coming from behind to win. The match was played despite the continuing lack of support and recognition from the SFA, exemplified by their chief executive, Willie Allen, who, in a newspaper interview about the match stated that the SFA did not approve of ladies playing football. The effort it took to organise the match, select and train the Scottish team, find kit and promote the match is testament to Elsie's commitment to the cause. She was supported in this by her friendship with Pat Gregory who was then secretary of the English WFA – a friendship that has lasted across the years and was demonstrated so well in the UEFA-backed short film about the planning of the 1972 international.

Although the SWFA worked hard to persuade the SFA to remove restrictions on women's football, this had little impact on the SFA. When the SFA agreed on 29 August 1974 to give recognition to women's football, the drivers for the decision were more likely pressure from UEFA and the potential impact from the Sex Discrimination Act 1975 and the requirement for equal provision of goods and services. This would have ended the SFA's ability to demand that its member clubs and officials stopped women from using their facilities and services.

Elsie was still involved with domestic football having moved to Westthorn United, a team that included Edna Neillis, one of the best players of that generation. After the lifting of restrictions on women's football, Elsie helped to organise one of two matches that took place in football stadiums ahead of European cup ties. One was at Tannadice Stadium in Dundee between Dundee United and East Fife. The other tool place on

18 September 1974 at Celtic Park when Westthorn United played Stewarton Thistle in front of a full house ahead of their cup tie match against Olympiacos. For the women on these teams, the matches afforded them a glimpse of playing football within the male infrastructure. Margaret McAulay (Captain of Westthorn United and Scotland) recalled that she and Edna Neillis, who were both Glasgow Rangers fans, vowed not to celebrate if they scored for Westthorn as this would be in front of fans of a rival club. However, on the night, as Margaret passed the ball to Edna who scored, neither could resist wheeling away in celebration to the roars of the Celtic Park crowd. Elsie later recalled that Jock Stein, then manager at Celtic was a strong advocate for the women's game and had stood at the entrance to the tunnel and clapped the women off as they left the pitch.

Elsie had been finding combining the work as SWFA secretary with her other commitments a challenge. This was not just about time constraints but also all the paperwork she had at home as there was no SWFA office at this point. However, when she resigned from the role at a board meeting, she was taken aback to be offered the role of manager of the team. She agreed to do this for a short period.

It is not clear exactly when she took over but Elsie was in charge of the Scotland team that played two matches in Italy in September 1974, with the hosts covering their expenses to enable them to travel. The second match was played at the San Siro stadium, Milan, and women involved that day recalled being overwhelmed by the venue, the welcome they received and the positive attitude to women's football.

Elsie also managed the team for a memorable match against Northern Ireland in November 1974 which saw the side win 11-1. However, Elsie had faced some criticism about her team selection in Italy and at the end of 1974 resigned her role, in frustration at what she saw as the inward-looking attitude of the board. There was then a falling out and disagreement which ultimately led to three of the most significant women in the Scotland team, Elsie Cook, Rose Reilly and Edna Neillis being stopped from playing in or for Scotland *sine die* (indefinitely/ without end).

Elsie dropped out of frontline work once she was disqualified *sine die* by the SWFA, but her passion for the game saw her coaching girls' teams as these developed with the slow but steady growth of women's football. Interest in her work in the 1970s grew as writing about women's football grew in the late 1990s. This interest has steadily grown and as well as having taken part in radio and TV programmes, documentaries and newspaper and magazine articles, she now works with the SFA and SWF to promote the game and celebrate the women who have played for Scotland since 1972.

THE THREAD OF TEAMS IN WOMEN'S FOOTBALL IN SCOTLAND FROM THE 1960S TO THE END OF THE 1990S
Karen Fraser

THE SEARCH FOR INFORMATION on women's football can be challenging at times and so this should be viewed as an introduction or an outline sketch of the thread of women's teams through the 40 years from 1960 to 2000. The intention is that this thread will be strengthened and expanded over time. Through this period of time, there have been teams playing in a variety of different settings. Teams that played with just the handful of other teams they were aware of, those that played in local galas and tournaments, teams that participated in the leagues and competitions set up by the Scottish Women's Football Association (SWFA) and teams that played within the more informal leagues and competitions that took place across the whole country. If the information about the domain covered by the SWFA is at times limited, then the informal area is even more challenging to explore. There has been work on this but so far there is more detail about the earlier years.

1960 to 1974

Through the work of a handful of researchers, the message is starting to permeate that contrary to popular belief, Scottish women's football did not suddenly emerge fully formed in the late 1990s as the Scottish Football Association became officially involved. Rather, women have played football in Scotland for a very long time and ongoing research suggests this was in far greater numbers than may have been thought.

Initially, writing about Scottish women's football in the 1960s centred on a handful of teams with some fabulous names:

Cambuslang Hooverettes
Fife Dynamites
Glasgow Gay XI
Holyrood Bumbees
Johnstone Red Rockets
Stewarton Thistle
Tayside Toppers

The teams below are those that were invited to join the first unofficial league in Scotland in 1968 and 1969:

Aberdeen Prima Donnas
Cambuslang Hooverettes
Dundee Strikers
Edinburgh Dynamos
Motherwell AEI
Stewarton Thistle
Westthorn United
(who were the Glasgow Gay XI)

By 1972 and the formation of the SWFA, other teams were emerging and some of the original names appeared less frequently.

Official League Founder Members	Joined By
Aberdeen Prima Donnas	Arbroath LFC
Dundee Strikers	Dunfermline LFC
Edinburgh Dynamos	East Fife
Motherwell AEI	Harmony Row
Stewarton Thistle	Monklands LFC
Westthorn United	West End LFC

The information above shows a total of twelve teams identified in connection with the SWFA league and recorded in previous writing. However, research into the period up to 1974, undertaken just prior to the compilation of this book, has shown that this is to seriously underestimate the amount of football being played by women at this time. The research has so far identified a further 60 teams playing at that time and some of these are listed below with the names showing the spread of teams across much of the country:

Aberdeen Ladies FC
Airdrie Ladies FC
Alexander Bus Company LFC
Alford Amazons
Arbroath LFC
Ayr Rebels
Baxter's Belles
Black Rock Belles
Braemar Caledonians
Cove Rangers Ladies
Cross & Blackwell's Women
Cummins Engine Ladies FC

Dunfermline Ladies
Dykehead and Shotts Co-op
East Fife
Elm Tree Ladies
Forres Flamingos
Friockheim Fireballs
Harmony Row
Hills Coupons Ltd
Huntley Hotshots
Kingussie Snowdrops
Littlewoods Stores
Levi's Ladies
Livingston Inn Ladies
Lossie Lambs
MacFisheries Ladies
Mayflower Babes
Metal Box Pirates
Monklands LFC
Nairn Kestrels
Pittenweem Panthers
Red Devils Grantown
Tarves Women
Timex Tickers
West End FC Ladies

It should be noted that at present these teams are gleaned from newspapers that have been digitised and so only represent a small number of geographical areas. It would be likely that this is replicated across the country and mean there are many more teams to identify. This is particularly likely as many of the teams are connected to workplaces.

Many of these teams will have only played occasionally for charity matches or gala days and this is a pattern repeated across the 30 years. Equally, some of these teams played frequently and regularly with a number appearing in the SWFA leagues across decades. Work is underway to further expand this list.

In September 1972, the SWFA was formed and a more formal structure emerged with a league and official cup competitions. However, there was a large unofficial sphere outside the control of the SWFA and numerous leagues and tournaments took place with a very large number of teams participating. Many of the reports in the papers in the early 1970s refer to tournaments as part of gala days or charity matches. Examples include an eight-team tournament in Turriff in Aberdeenshire to raise money for the town's swimming pool fund and the Arbroath FC Supporters Club Ladies Football Cup which appears to have run for at least two years in the early 1960s.

1974 to 2000

For a number of reasons, unconnected to women's football, in 1974, the SFA finally got in line with the rest of UEFA and lifted the restrictions on women's football. However, for most women playing this had little initial impact, especially as the game was not supported or encouraged. This meant that while conditions were a little easier for the SWFA, the challenging terms set for affiliation to the SFA meant that they were unable to unlock the advantages this would bring.

The SWFA was keen to make sure that women's football in Scotland had the opportunity to grow, even though their official domestic reach was limited. As a result, they were supportive of the growing unofficial sphere of Scottish women's football as they were aware of the importance of matches to players.

This unofficial sphere included local leagues, such as the Strathclyde League, locally organised tournaments and gala days. As well as increasing the games available to all teams they also enabled the development of teams to a point where they felt able to join an official league.

Within both the official and unofficial spheres what was

important to the women was the opportunity to play – and so there were a number of football formats adopted to expand playing opportunities. Women's football in Scotland appears to have embraced the five-a-side format with much enthusiasm. The format was popular because it required fewer players and was predominantly held indoors, which meant better playing conditions and less weather-related disruption – a definite bonus in Scotland! The distinctive style of play of five-a-side football also enabled different teams to experience winning.

The origins of teams continued to be mixed – they may have been an existing team, a mix of two teams or a new team formed by friends, participants of another team sport such as hockey or netball or workplace teams. Research into this is still in the early stages however, research into this area has provided small leads into a different aspect of workplace teams – those that played exclusively 'internally'. That is, larger workplaces that had their own football leagues, including for women's football. Fiona, who played in the later 1980s and went on to both referee and work with the SWFA explained her route into a league team:

> So, it was probably around 1987, maybe 1988 when I worked for the Royal Bank of Scotland and they were doing a football tournament and they had a ladies' section. So, being the type of person, I am, of course I had to try and get a team together and talked some friends I worked with into playing football...We played and we were actually quite successful. We won a couple of bank tournaments and inter-bank tournaments.

This suggests that there was sufficient interest in women's football within banks to have internal and external tournaments. There is little further information at present but the experience led to Fiona joining a team that was in the second division of the SWFA leagues and this may well have been the gateway to playing football for other women.

Although a large number of teams have been found playing in the unofficial sphere in the 1960 to 1974 period, research into this later period has not found so much detail as yet. However, the records of the SWFA do provide details of the fluctuations in team numbers in the 'official' sphere from 1974 to 2000. As can be seen from the diagrams below, there was an upsurge in the number of leagues and therefore teams in the official sphere, from the early 1990s. This was in part due to funding from Sportscotland which enabled the creation of a role of Development Officer to grow the game for women and girls.

As the number and size of leagues grew, so the need for tournaments to provide extra games declined. While there is still more information to uncover, there appears to have been a peak of additional tournaments in the 1980s. At this time, in addition to league games, teams could be involved in:

A pre-season tournament in Dundee
The league cup for their division
The Scottish Cup
A mid-season tournament in Paisley
The end of season Leven Cup
Two national 5-a-side tournaments and
Many other local tournaments

Recognising the importance of competitions to teams and players, the SWFA worked hard to ensure that competitions arranged by them and other organisations, continued to run for as long as possible. As part of this, the SWFA did not prevent teams that were members from taking part in events that were not backed by the SWFA. In 1974, the SWFA worked with Leven Town Council to organise an end-of-season tournament.

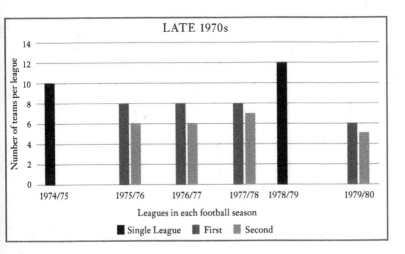

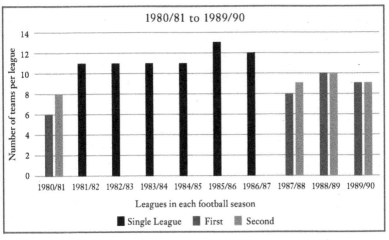

The first Leven Tournament was held in June 1974, and whilst organised via the entertainment rather than sports department, the tournament was taken seriously by the council who funded it for a further 22 years.

It appears that the upsurge in the number of teams and leagues from the early 1990s began to negate the need for large numbers of additional competitions and over time the official SWFA tournaments were the Scottish Cup and the League Cup.

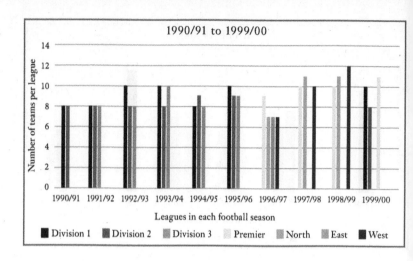

Conclusion

At the moment much of this detail is sparse: a team name, where they played and an estimate of how long the team lasted. More information is slowly being added but it is a large and ongoing project.

A CURLER TO REMEMBER

Peter Clive

'In life, as in art,
the beautiful moves in curves':
a change of pace,
a change of direction;
she sends the defender the wrong way;
she sees the chance and takes it,
putting such a spin on the ball
with the side of her foot
the air itself takes part
and curls it into the corner
of the net, in life, as in art.

ROSE REILLY
Fiona Skillen & Karen Fraser

BORN IN KILMARNOCK and brought up in Stewarton in Ayrshire, Rose Reilly always loved football. When Rose was five, she wrote a letter to Santa Claus asking for a football of her own but she was disappointed when she received a doll. This did not stop her though and she found a small boy with a football who was prepared to swap it for the doll. That ball became her cherished possession, taken everywhere with her.

Rose was determined to play football at any cost despite the dismay and disapproval of her parents. She had such natural talent that at six she was asked by the manager of the Stewarton Boy's Club to play for the team. She was delighted but there was a catch, she had to get her hair cut and call herself Ross. She went ahead and had her hair cut even though she knew her mum would be very angry. What mattered was that Rose now had a football kit, even if she had to get dressed in it at home as she could not get changed with the boys in their changing room. Her ability to score goals brought her to the attention of a Celtic scout who watched her run rings round the opposition and score eight goals. The scout told the manager he wanted to sign the wee lad who had scored all the goals but changed his mind when he learnt that Ross was actually Rose. Rose was gutted and thought that if she was good enough what did it matter that she was a girl.

When she was seven, she approached Elsie Cook, the manager of the recently formed women's team, Stewarton Thistle and asked to play. She was told to come back two years later, which she did, exactly two years later to the day.

Rose was an all-round gifted athlete, excelling at pentathlon and at sixteen was picked in the Scotland training squad for the Edinburgh 1970 Commonwealth Games.

Football, however, was her first love and this is where she

focused her efforts. This led to her being expelled from secondary school for playing football, meaning that teenage Rose ended up taking a job in a carpet factory in Kilmarnock. She hated it but it allowed her to play football and plan for the future.

Stewarton Thistle were one of the top teams playing in Scotland at the time and with them Rose took part in the unofficial league started in 1969 and a number of tournaments. These included the Butlin's Cup, a women's football tournament started by the television personality Hughie Green where Stewarton reached the regional final. Rose was part of the Stewarton side which lifted the inaugural Scottish Cup in 1971 and also reached the final of the inaugural English Women's Football Association Cup (Mitre Cup) the same year.

In 1972, she and Elsie moved to Westthorn United to play alongside Edna Neillis and Margaret McAulay who were two of the best players in the country. This line-up made Westthorn United a formidable side and with them Rose won the treble of Scottish Cup, League Cup and the first League championship. Westthorn also reached the English WFA Cup final although they lost to Southampton, just as Stewarton Thistle had done.

Rose also starred for Scotland in the historic first international match against England in 1972, a match described elsewhere in the book. Rose has said that it was a very proud moment to put on the Scotland shirt and also to score in the historic game. She said that nothing is better than representing your country at the game you love.

Rose knew that playing football was all she wanted to do but at that time, there was no way for girls to make football a career in the UK. Her mile and a half walk to work allowed her space to think. It was during this walk that she conjured up a plan to make her footballing dream a reality. In 1974, with assistance from teammates, she managed to get sponsored by her local newspaper, The *Daily Record*, and travelled to France for a trial at Reims. Seventeen-year-old Rose's talent shone bright and she was signed at half-time!

After a six-month spell with Reims, which included winning a league title, Rose signed for AC Milan. There she played for the women's professional team for four years, winning her first two league titles in the process. She taught herself Italian within a year, using a dictionary to read the daily football paper, chatting to teammates and locals and immersing herself in the Italian way of life.

After her time at Milan, Rose continued to play in Italy for Catania, Lecce Napoli and Fiorentina across the next two decades, winning a further six league titles. Reilly twice won the Serie A Golden Boot during seasons 1978 and 1981, scoring 43 and 45 goals respectively (including those scored in the Italian Cup).

In the 1978/79 season, she was contacted by her former club, Reims in France, and asked to come back. Rose did not want to leave Italy and so did both – playing for Lecce on a Saturday night before flying to France to play for Reims on Sunday afternoons. Remarkably both of the clubs won their respective league titles meaning that Rose won two championships in a season!

Despite having played for the Scottish national side on a number of occasions and continuing to be one of the best Scottish women footballers at the time, Rose did not play for Scotland after her move. This is because she, Edna Neillis and Elsie Cook were all banned *sine die* by the Scottish Women's Football Association (SWFA). There had been criticism of the SWFA and although not exactly clear, as both this public criticism and turning professional have been cited as reasons for the ban. Whatever the reason, Rose was not in the country and was not even aware of the ban.

This did not end her international career, however. She was a huge hit in Italy's Serie A, and she was asked by the country's

President to play for the Italian national team. She agreed and captained the side thirteen times. She was selected to captain Italy in the Mundialito, the unofficial Women's World Cup in 1984, scoring in a 3–1 win over Germany in the final. She was also voted the Italian team's best player. Rose was also named female world footballer of the year, and became a household name in her adopted homeland.

She eventually retired aged 40.

In 2007, she was inducted into the Scottish Football Hall of Fame and became the first female recipient of a PFA Scotland Merit Award in 2011. Rose was awarded an MBE in the 2020 New Year Honours for services to women's football.

There is also a sports centre named after her in Stewarton where young girls can play football. She continues to be a proud and active ambassador for the women's game in Scotland.

BY ONY ITHER NAME

Thomas Clark

The scouts wir left staunin. Defenders, the same,
When the seventh flew in in the unner eights game;
'Haw, gie us a bell when thon Ross laddie grows!'
Yon scouts are still waitin. Yon laddie wis Rose.

Rose Reilly, Rose Reilly, yer feet are sae fleet,
Ye megged aw the laddies an made thaim tae greet;
The boys that wir chasin ye hadnae a chance,
Rose Reilly, Rose Reilly, ye led thaim a dance!

They tried tae disguise ye wi short back an sides,
But yer smarts wir the staun-oot that nae man
    could hide;
Nae dummy wis spat when they gied ye a doll,
Ye jist went doon the playgrund an swapped for a
ball.

Rose Reilly, Rose Reilly, the tanner baw Pele,
They gied ye the belt an they prayed tae expel ye;
The heidies wir haundin doon ban efter ban,
But Rose Reilly, Rose Reilly, wis aff tae Milan!

It's easy tae caw it the muive o yer dreams
When ye stairt aff in Stewarton, wind up in Reims;
But this wis yer hame, an ye'd mebbe hiv steyed
If the pouers-that-be wir the pouers-that-peyed.

Rose Reilly, Rose Reilly, yer name micht be flouery,
But yer hert wis like ice when ye wore the Azzurri;
Lionesses noo rampant wir jist wakin up,
Rose Reilly, Rose Reilly, had won the Warld Cup!

The pageant, the contest, the lycra-tight figure,
The warld then was sma; but you made it bigger.
They banned ye fae fitba for sweet SFA,
But nae goalie could stop ye, an neither could they.

Rose Reilly, Rose Reilly, the fix wis aye in,
Short skirts for the lassies, twa points for the win;
But the net couldnae haud ye, ye shot throu the waw,
Rose Reilly, Rose Reilly, the belle o the baw!

GAME CHANGERS

Shaun Moore

In the game of beauty, statistics are vital,
And we love wur lists, The Greatest Evers,
Not just the showy, silky sensations, but
The bad and the ugly, the hackers and cluggers.

Cite old midfield generals, perpetuate,
Mythical heroes and hardmen and postulate,
Recall the enforcers to the old debate,
Naming the not so good and the great.

  The rock, the anchor, one in every team,
  Tell us, who's the toughest you've seen?

Then cynical trip on the field of memories,
A deliberate dive down memory lane,
Memories tugged like shirts in the box,
Taking the offending names.

  Famous axemen, psychos, hatchets and bams?
  Old tales of aggression we've heard at length?
NO! let's discern between who was plain
  mental,
    . . . And who showed a mental strength.

  Aye, different kinds of acts of courage.
  Tell us, who had...character?

A resilience born of resistance,
A bravery based on bottle not brawn,
Who tied up their mouldies and pulled up their socks,
And dug in their heels cos they were thrawn.

Stood up to the masters of the House On The Hill,
Excluded from academy or school,
Insulted, questioned by virtue of sex,
Sexualised objects of ridicule.

Performed with grace under parental pressure,
Withstood the pressure of peers,
Made a stand without the home support,
Didn't sign up for the prescribed careers.

Outside, Left on the fringes,
Of the regulation social scene,
No sweepers of hearths or keepers of homes,
But keepers of goals and dreams.

For nurturing dreams of raising cups,
Aspiring to more than Trophy Bride,
Because they didn't follow that game plan,
Slagged for playing for the other side.

Refused to know their Carlton Place,
Breached the defensive Park Gardens wall,
Tore up the old boys' club roll of dishonour,
Showed backbone. Showed heart. Showed balls.

> None of them household names,
> But players that changed the game.

LYNN FORSYTH
Richard S Young

IN THE LONG heat wave summer of 1984, I encountered Lynn Forsyth for the first time. We were both members of Clydesdale Cricket Club on Glasgow's southside with myself as a cricketer and Lynn as a hockey player with Glasgow Western.

As an eighteen-year-old, I had become ensorcelled by this diminutive Amazonian powerhouse that loved all sports and always had a smile on her face. I'll be honest enough to admit that I had always viewed women in sport with a typically sexist attitude and that my interest was always somewhat questionable.

It was a Monday evening and I was practising cricket on the outfield with some friends when Lynn walked over to us, picked a cricket ball up and asked if she could bowl a few. We agreed and quickly realised that her bowling was very good and perhaps better than some of our peers. She asked us if we were doing anything that evening and did we play football? We said that we could and I remember her reply as if it was yesterday: 'Good. I'm three short for a mixed hockey game tonight and I need players. Don't worry about not having played hockey before because it is just football but using your hands and a stick instead of your feet. You guys use cricket bats to hit the ball. I just need you to use a stick instead'.

We agreed to play and during that match I changed my perception and yes, I admit prejudice about women in sport. It might have been Lynn nutmegging me with the hockey ball and whispering 'choo-choo' as she ghosted past me or afterwards watching her playing keepie-uppie with a football. I was lucky if I could do ten or so but she was in overdrive and was well into the 50s.

We became great friends thereafter and I learned that she was a dual internationalist at both football and hockey with 68 caps for hockey alone. She would have been a triple internationalist at cricket had the women's game been developed enough back then.

The years passed and to be honest I hadn't seen or spoken to Lynn for about 30 years or so. I had got involved with the #Fitba150 project and that part of that was showcasing women's football. I suggested to Professor Fiona Skillen that Lynn Forsyth would be a great study to have at the first event on 17 November 2022 at Clydesdale Cricket Club – Fiona agreed and I made contact with Lynn and explained the evening to her.

I met Lynn before the evening started. The passing of time had not stopped us from continuing from where we had left off – as good friends who shared a passion for sport.

Lynn was interviewed in front of a packed Clydesdale clubhouse as she told her sporting adventures to the audience. The warmth of appreciation was evident and Lynn shone as she revealed her unique story – she had only been fifteen when she was picked to play for Scotland at football, and at the time, was also the youngest ever internationalist – she scored four goals on her debut against Ireland. A huge cheer rang out from the audience as they also clapped their appreciation for her efforts.

A year later in December 2023, Lynn was invited to Hampden to the Scotland vs England women's fixture and to finally receive her cap for football, nearly 50 years after making her debut. She was joined on the evening with a host of other women who were also there to receive their international caps and recognition retrospectively. And rightly so – they represented their country and were finally being acknowledged.

Words cannot describe the pride and joy I felt for Lynn when she finally got her football cap. Fully deserved and a just reward for a woman who has been a perfect ambassador for sport in general and engaging everyone to participate in and enjoy.

FLEETS

Stuart Paterson
For Julie Fleeting

You put the start to finish
winning into Kilwinning
jumped in the air
but never the river for Ayr
ran hundreds of netstretching runners
for London's Gunners
briefly but valiantly
goalgettingly pure for Valur
put go in goals and San Diego
first to last minutes for the Spirits
won games as a fleeting
boss bounty for Ross County
were Lassie and Bhoy in every
heartfelt kick for Celtic
kicks flicks magic tricks
goalscoringly gritty for Glasgow City
never the flower but always our
Power of Scotland

THE WOMEN BEFORE HER

Julie McNeill

Not yet six
she half sits,
half stands

her body fizzing
fixated on the pink
shirts before her.

She's singing for
Shelley's army and
doesn't miss a beat

eighteen thousand
voices, for our
girls, for our game

for her Scotland.
They show her
what women

can do when
we raise each other.
She believes in

the women who
save themselves,
the girls standing

ready to gie it laldy
shoulder to shoulder
before her.

SHELLEY KERR
Julie McNeill

SHELLEY KERR's journey in football began like many others: with a passion for the game and a drive to succeed against the odds. Born and raised in Scotland, her love for the game ignited at an early age but few might have predicted just how far she would go.

She will forever be synonymous with that wave of positivity and sisterhood that seemed to sweep across Scotland during the qualifiers and tournament of the FIFA Women's World Cup France 2019™ Young girls singing 18,000 strong at Hampden Park for Shelley's army as they played Jamacia before travelling to France to compete is a moment which will live long in the memory of any fan of football or champion of equality.

Her love of the game started way before 2019 though. As a young girl, Shelley showed exceptional talent on the football pitch, drawing attention for her natural athleticism and technical prowess. Her big breakthrough came when she was selected to represent Scotland at international level. Her performances on the field were always a heady blend of skill, dogged tenacity and strong leadership, earning her respect and admiration from opponents and teammates.

Despite facing numerous challenges and obstacles throughout her playing career, from entrenched gender biases to limited resources and opportunities for female athletes she remained undaunted, channelling her determination into overcoming adversity and striving for excellence on the football pitch.

Shelley played football for various clubs throughout her career, both domestically and internationally as well as representing Scotland in the Scottish Women's National Team. She had stints with several clubs in the Scottish Women's Premier League, including Kilmarnock and Hearts and joined clubs in England, such as Arsenal Ladies. Her time at Arsenal was particularly successful, as she played a key role in the team's triumphs in domestic and international competitions.

Despite retiring from playing, Kerr's passion for the game endured, leading her to transition into coaching – a decision that would further solidify her legacy in football. As a coach, she continued to break new ground, imparting her knowledge and experience to the next generation of players.

Her impact on women's football extends beyond the pitch. As the head coach of the Scottish Women's National Team, she spearheaded a resurgence in interest and participation in the sport. Under her stewardship, the team achieved unprecedented success, qualifying for the 2019 FIFA Women's World Cup in France – a historic milestone for Scottish women's football.

Against a backdrop of fervent anticipation and heightened expectations, Kerr led her team with poise and determination on the world stage. While the tournament presented formidable challenges, including strong opponents and intense scrutiny, her unwavering belief in her team's abilities instilled confidence and resilience.

Despite facing setbacks and narrow defeats, the team's spirited performances captured the hearts of football enthusiasts worldwide, cementing their place as formidable contenders on the global stage.

Beyond the tournament itself, Shelley Kerr's presence and influence resonated as a catalyst for change within the broader landscape of women's football. Her relentless advocacy for gender equality and equal opportunities sparked important conversations and inspired future generations of female athletes to pursue their dreams without inhibition or constraint.

She is an important catalyst for change and stands as a transformative figure in the realm of women's football. From her pioneering days as a player to her trailblazing time as a coach, she has consistently championed the cause of women's football with unwavering passion and dedication. As the sport continues to evolve and flourish, Shelley Kerr's place in the history books will undoubtedly endure as a symbol of inspiration and empowerment for generations to come.

She serves as a testament to the transformative potential of women's football, the determination of women to rise against the odds and the enduring impact of those who dare to dream and defy expectations.

ERIN

Jim Mackintosh

Yesterday, a long time ago
we shared your joy
and felt your pain.

Anytime, from now on
it will be okay to do the same.
We're signed up.

You fell from scoring highs
to the foetal-curl of loss
and shared your despair
– the pitch was your pillow.

Yet you stood up
in the razor glare
of unforgiving media scrutiny
– a nation's arm around you.

And standing on a knife edge
wanting be anywhere
you already looked wiser.

'Don't give up on your dreams.
I've achieved mine.'
– we understood

This wasn't it.
This was only another milestone.
Erin. We thank you.

MOTHER TONGUE

Stephen Watt

Anthills of people surge the escalator,
pathologically patting passports
placed in rear squares of denim.

She is leaving this hustle. Bustle. *Disco
Inferno*. Sweet grape-words she uses, now,
will shrivel. Become raisin on her tongue.
But the seeds of new words will come.

Tiny suitcases trundle past, strapped
with cuddly toy lions and giraffes.
Their warm, safari-tanned faces
beam like bedside lamps

          and she is caught off-guard
remembering Mum's *Scone Palace* apron
which hung permanently
from her bedroom door hook.
She gave her it as a keepsake
to never forget her roots;
the red sandstones of her childhood.

Doubt burns. Pushing hesitation
like frantic vending machines,
she wants to split herself in two. Not miles
from the lifestyle she once knew
but in a place like home, where dust and love
are ingrained in the grooves.

Clouds offer the unknown.

In this alien land of wild garlic
and green cuckoo, she chants her talent
in lush gardens. Each bend and swoop
translates foreign autumns
into the universal language
of orbiting satellites

and when the ball sings on her laces,
she hears it loud and clearly
in her mother tongue;
You – have – arrived.

NOTE:

With special thanks to Lana Clelland for her input to this poem.

147

WHO SAYS?

Tom Murray

I could never get my head around this mush
about who gets to do what!
Who says?
I mean there's no extra time in this game.
Once your whistle blows you leave the field.
If your thing is keepy uppy in your back garden,
dreaming of World Cup glory, when a wee lassie,
who says you can't dream?
Who says only boys cross the touchline to reality?
There's things to be worried about in this life.
Lassies playing football isn't one of them.
The field's big enough for dreams a plenty.

Scotland

This section of the book reflects on the importance of Scotland's National Team, their successes and the influence they have had on our nation. From the first 'unofficial' international of 1972 through to our most recent games at Hampden via the excitement of qualifying for our first major tournament, the 2017 European Championships, and our thrilling qualification for our first ever World Cup in 2019.

A LEGACY TO CHERISH
Steven Lawther

THE PATH OF the Scotland Women's National Team towards their first ever major tournament was long, arduous and littered with painful moments. The conceding of a goal to Spain with the last kick of the ball in the second leg of a 2013 European Championship play-off, when the squad were on the very brink of qualification, encapsulated the frustration and may have persuaded even the most ardent Scotland supporter to give up hope.

Yet, one person never lost belief – Scotland manager Anna Signeul. 'Anna always knew that we would make it across the line', reflects former Scotland defender, Joelle Murray. 'We thought it would always be that typical, Scottish hard-luck story, but Anna came in with such a positive attitude. As time went on, we bought into her belief, her confidence, and her positivity.'

Swedish born Signeul, along with her assistant, Ann-Hélen Grahm, embraced the adversity and moulded it to an advantage. 'They taught the squad what we needed to know through that journey', says former Scotland player, Leanne Crichton. 'As much as those individual moments were tough, I think we needed to go through that to know what it takes to overcome it the next time.'

'Those moments weren't easy', agrees Murray. 'It was very raw. You did have doubt and negative thoughts, but the people that Anna and Ann-Hélen were, they didn't let us dwell on anything. It was immediately, "How can we improve? How can we be better?"'

The reward for this self-reflection and perseverance was qualification for the 2017 European Championships, their first ever appearance at a major tournament. An achievement quickly followed by qualification for their first ever World Cup in 2019 under Signeul's successor, Shelley Kerr.

'It was such a proud moment', says Joelle Murray. 'It was a moment that you always dreamt about. The joy and excitement of being able to share it with people who were not only teammates but friends as well. It was incredibly special.'

'It wasn't just about one person's journey or you as an individual', agrees Crichton. 'It was about the players that had been there, done it, and had faced so many disappointments. Players like Gemma Fay, Jo Love, Ifeoma Dieke, players that had amassed hundreds of caps for Scotland. It was a whole nation that had worked for decades to get us there. We were just the lucky ones.'

Appearing at two successive tournaments had an immediate impact, accelerating the profile of the Scotland squad and bringing attention that pioneers of the women's game could only have dreamed about. 'You almost instantly felt a shift in the mindset in terms of the culture of the women's game and the way people were speaking about the women's game', explains Crichton. 'I think you were perceived in a different way and on a different level. People spoke about women footballers not just girls who play football.'

It also brought an increased confidence on the pitch and belief in Scotland as a strong footballing nation. 'You started to feel a parity with other nations even just to be there', says Crichton. 'Scotland was always that team that was so near yet so far, or had individuals such as Kim Little, a world class player but had never been at a major tournament. There was that level of insecurity, but when you get to that level and that stage, it puts a lot of stuff to bed. It reassures you.'

If there was hope that the experience would allow Scotland to push on and become regulars at big tournaments, it was not realised. The side fell short in qualification for both the 2022 European Championships and the 2023 World Cup and under new manager Pedro Martínez Losa are currently trying to recapture that winning formula.

'We have been trying to find an identity over the last couple of years', says Joelle Murray. 'There has been a lot of transition, players in, players out and I think it is only recently that we are finding a style or a consistent team or continuity. There has been a lot of moving parts and it has been a pretty tough period for the national team. I'd like to think now there is a core group of players that can really drive the team forward and play the way that Pedro and his staff want to play.'

If events on-field have been difficult in the last few years, off the pitch, frustrations also exist. The previous generation of women footballers faced significant obstacles to play the game, break down barriers and receive respect and recognition for their efforts. Frustratingly, this type of battle appears to persist, with ongoing disputes around the level of support and investment provided to the national squad.

'It seems like yesterday that prior to the Euros in 2017 we were having the same discussions and the same disputes', says Joelle Murray. 'That is six years now that these issues have been rumbling on in the background and players are fighting for things that they ultimately feel that they don't have. That is disappointing. You see other nations ensuring their women's team are supported and have everything that they need to be at their peak on the pitch.'

'It all comes down to investment', suggests Leanne Crichton. 'If you look at Spain, a side we beat in 2017 at the Euros, and their development and progress since. There are a lot of the same players we played that night, there have not been wholesale changes in that side and then you look at our national team. I think a lot of the issue is you don't have the same financial resource. Missing out on qualification has a huge impact on the revenue we generate. That is why it is so important that we get back to qualifying for major tournaments.'

If the promise of qualification has not been fully realised, the legacy of participation 2017 and 2019 does endure. Murray and Crichton experience this first-hand as they nurture younger players at their respective clubs – Hibernian and Motherwell. 'I think of the level of investment in the top clubs in Scotland, you can see that shift in mentality', says Crichton. 'When you look at the academy structures at most clubs, including here at Motherwell, it has made a real difference. There is a pathway for girls and women to see.'

'Young Scotland midfielder Kirsty MacLean is a great example', continues Crichton. 'She was able to see and become invested in a team that had been at a major tournament and as a young aspiring footballer says, "I want to be that and I know I can be that because I have now got the tools to go and apply myself at my club and invest in my future". There is a real vision there now.'

'Young players need role models to look up to', agrees Murray. 'We are fortunate to have had Caroline Weir in our academy, Kim Little in our academy and multiple players who are now playing at the top, top level of the game. Young players see that link and it help show what you can achieve by being at a club like Hibs. These players have been there and walked in their shoes and now Caroline is at Real Madrid and Kim Little has been all over the world and is now playing at a top club like Arsenal. Young girls can look to them and see a great advert for playing professional women's football.'

Where once players had to pay to play, argue for unpaid leave from work, or build their career around a job that could accommodate the demands of international football, there is now opportunity and the prospect of full-time contracts.

'When you start playing football', says Murray. 'You don't do it for any other reason than you love the game and have a passion for the game, but it is fantastic to see that more opportunities now coming and players being rewarded with contracts, sponsorship, and partnership deals.'

Joelle Murray and Leanne Crichton may no longer be able

to influence things on the field for the Scotland Women's National Team, but they are both committed to doing what they can to support the squad.

'The decision (to retire) can be quite tough one', explains Murray. 'It is raw and hard at times to take in and reflect on, but I enjoy watching the games now, doing the commentary on the games and I do still have friends within that squad who I enjoy seeing being in that environment and thriving. I do feel there is an onus there to push the game forward.'

'When you have been a player for a huge number of years', adds Crichton. 'You have always been able to influence things. It is tough to watch because you want to be part of it, you want to be in amongst it and helping make it better. I'm sure every former player probably feels the same way. All you can do now is support them, elevate them, and speak about them.'

The Scotland Women's National Team that Murray and Crichton were part of provided us with some very special moments to cherish and a legacy for those that followed. The hope is that future squads can seize their opportunity to do the same.

SCOTLAND'S WOMEN'S FIRST
INTERNATIONAL
Karen Fraser

REFERENCES TO MATCHES involving Scotland and England appear all the way back to 1881 but the majority of these are existing teams that happen to be from the two countries, rather than teams selected from players within the country. This can be seen from the 'international' promoted in 1881 through tours of Scotland by English teams across the twentieth century.

Although there was a significant amount of women's football played in the 1960s, there was no formal infrastructure to support the formation of a national team. However, there continued to be the marketing of matches between teams from each of the countries to stimulate interest. For example, when the Butlin's Cup was started in 1969, the whole tournament was structured to ensure a 'Scotland vs England' final. The teams were in fact club sides from the two countries but this was a marketing ploy seeking to set up the type of Scotland verses England rivalry seen in the men's game to build interest and audiences.

In 1969, before the associations in England or Scotland had recognised women's football, Stewarton Thistle played the Manchester Corinthians in England. Elsie Cook wanted to invite the team to Scotland but also wanted to make sure they had suitable opponents. To do this, she decided to put together a Scotland Select team and invited a number of Scottish teams to come through to Stewarton for trials and the strongest XI was picked by two ex-professionals, Rab Stewart (Kilmarnock) and Billy Neil (Rangers). Manchester Corinthians played on behalf of England to play the first ever 'selected' Scottish team. Elsie said it was a cracking game and although Scotland were beaten 3–1 it showed what women could accomplish and that they could play football well.

Following the formation of the Scottish Women's Football Association (SWFA) in 1972, it was decided that a great way to promote and demonstrate interest in women's football would be to organise the first official women's International between Scotland and England. Elsie, by then the SWFA secretary, liaised with Pat Gregory, her friend and counterpart from the English WFA, to organise the match which was held in Scotland in November that year. The women were responsible for arranging the stadium hire, travel, accommodation and other logistics.

With restrictions still in place in Scotland, the match could not be held on an association ground, and so Ravenscraig Park in Greenock was chosen. The venture had very little backing and even less funding and as a result just one week before the match, the jerseys were bought by Elsie from a jumble sale in Stewarton, using money donated by Rose Reilly's father. Elsie got her mother to take the jerseys to the knitwear factory she worked at and enlisted some of the women to help with sewing on the numbers. Elsie herself then sewed on the Scotland badge. The shorts and socks were loaned by Rangers Football Club.

Newspaper coverage of the upcoming match was scarce and what coverage there was focused on the women rather than the actual football played. One article appeared with the headline, above a picture of the team, 'Pretty impressive...the glory girls spurned by Scotland's soccer bosses'. As was common at the time, the article was not in the sports section and while it was generally supportive, there are indications that the women's game was not taken seriously. The headline leads with the word pretty to describe the team and then uses the term 'spurned', with its romantic connotations rather than the usual 'banned' or even shunned as was used in the article. The opening line reads, 'Here they are the pool for Scotland's latest International football team. Long glamourous hair, pretty plum lipstick and all'.

At this point, there was still no engagement with women's football by the Scottish Football Association and the article contains a rare insight into its view of women's football. This is contained in a quote from Willie Allen, the chief executive, who said, 'We just don't approve of ladies playing football'. Elsie said that the team was not taken seriously as many of the general population agreed with the SFA that football was not for women but the prejudice they faced just made them more determined to continue playing.

Players for Scotland were selected through a series of trials, held over a three-month period to form the strongest possible team. The squad for the match came from across five teams: Westthorn United (six players); Lees Ladies (three); Motherwell AEI (three); Dundee Strikers (three) and Cambuslang Hooverettes (one). The squad was guided by former Kilmarnock and St Mirren player, Rab Stewart, the first manager of the first Scotland Women's National Team.

Another aspect that fell to Elsie was arranging the training sessions for the squad and this did not always go smoothly. The final training session before the game was to be held at the ground but it nearly ended before it began. The girls were meeting up at Anderston Bus Station in Glasgow to be taken to the training venue together. Elsie recalled that one of the girls had offered to assist her by arranging the transport. However, it soon became clear that she had forgotten to do it and there was no transport. Elsie recalled trying to think what they could do and at that precise moment a furniture van pulled up at the traffic lights. Quick as a flash, Elsie ran to the van window and asked the help of the driver. In exchange for £30, he agreed to take them to Greenock in the back of the van which involved the team sitting on couches amongst the other furniture. Elsie said the women thought it was hilarious and it all added to the sense of adventure.

The match took place on 18 November 1972 in front of

400 spectators. The conditions during this match were far from ideal, as the pitch was frozen, and in the second half of the game, it snowed heavily. In the small amount of film available of the game the players and officials look frozen.

Scotland took the lead with Mary Carr and Rose Reilly scoring to make it 2–0 at half-time. Another player who was prominent in the match was Edna Neillis, who also went on to play professionally in France and Italy and was the female equivalent of Celtic's Jimmy Johnstone. However, during the second half, England managed to fight back, with Sylvia Gore scoring twice and Pat Davies once. As recalled by Elsie in her programme notes for a match against the Ladies Soccer League of Ireland in March 1974, 'Scotland were quickly up by 2 goals to nil. But as conditions deteriorated, in the second half, England came fighting back to win by 3 goals to 2, scoring the winner in the last three minutes'. Scotland and England have played each other a number of times since November 1972, with Scotland so far only recording one victory in 1977.

The 1972 team was captained by Margaret McAulay from Westthorn United and the full line-up, with pen pictures of the squad is given below. These are taken from the programme for the match:

Scotland
Colours: Navy/White, White Pants, Red Stockings
Houghton
Hunter   Hunter
Kidd   Mount   Walker
Reilly   Neillis   Anderson   McAulay (C)   Carr

Substitutes: Creamer, Davenport, Cooper, McLaren, Morrison

I would like to extend a warm welcome to our English guests this afternoon and hope their visit to Scotland may be an enjoyable one.

This being the first ever International between the two countries, I hope we shall have a good sporting game and be able to make this event an annual one.

R Stewart, Scotland Team Manager

Scotland Team

'Scotland are Captained today by Inside left Maragret McAulay (21), of Westthorn UTD, of Hamilton. Brilliant midfield player but prefers to bang in the goals. Janie Houghton (17), of Cambuslang Hooverettes is our goalkeeper and though rather short in stature for a keeper, is very agile and quick. Jean Hunter (17), part of the midfield trio of the successful Lees Ladies. Strong tackle and very able to take on a player or two by herself. June Hunter (19) is a very versatile player and can turn out in almost any position, Playing for Motherwell AEI and is today at Left Back. Linda Kidd (21), also of Lees Ladies. Linda comes from Kilmarnock. Good distributor of the ball and helps start many a dangerous attack. Marion Mount (18), Centre Half, plays for Westthorn Utd. Marion hails from Greenock so should be quite confident playing in front of her home crowd. Sandra Walker (22), of Lees Ladies, is married and has two young children. Sandra has it all, brilliant ball control, strong tackler, good header and the stylish arrogance of a Jim Baxter. Rose Reilly (17), perhaps the best-known of the Scots girls. Joint top goal scorer with the speed necessary in a winger and a terrific shot. Began her playing career when only seven years old for her local team Stewarton Thistle (now Lees Ladies). Has since joined Westthorn United. Edna Neillis (18). Brilliant ball-control and fantastic finish. Likened by many to

'Jinky' Johnstone of Celtic, which doesn't please Edna as she is a Rangers fanatic. A real character, joint top goal-scorer, plays for Westthorn Utd., easily distinguished by her red hair. Mary Anderson (18) also plays Centre Forward for her club, Westthorn Utd. Brilliant opportunist in front of goal. Mary Carr (20) plays on the left wing for her club, Motherwell AEI and lives in Hamilton. Liz Creamer (19), substitute goalkeeper, plays for Dundee Strikers. Mary Davenport (20), stocky defender who gives full ninety minutes. Plays for Westthorn Utd, and lives in Dunfermline. Linda Cooper (16) is the youngest member of the team. Turns out at Centre Forward for her club Dundee Strikers. Diane McLaren (17), also of Dundee Strikers, packs a strong shot and doesn't waste many chances. Irene Morrison (24), strong defender, usually plays centre half for her club, Motherwell AEI. Lets opponents know they have been in a game. Robert Stewart, Scottish Manager and former professional footballer with Kilmarnock and St Mirren.'

MATCHDAY

Maya Halcrow

I am the most sporty in my house
so it goes like this:
When its game day my Mum says:
'Come on we have to go.'
My Dad says:
'We've got plenty of time'.
I say:
'We are going to be so early again!'
Then my Dad jokes to my sister and says:
'You sure you don't want to come? I know how much
you love football.'
My sister grunts:
'Noooooooooooo!'
After the game my Dad says:
'You had better take those filthy boots off before you
get in my car.'
My Mum says:
'Remember to put your clothes in the wash when we
get home.'
My sister says:
'You are filthy and you stink!'
Soon after we arrive home I get changed,
forget what my mum had said and dump my clothes
on the floor.

THE STEEL VEINED PIONEERS

Jim Mackintosh

Raven's Cliff. On the Clyde's bending edge, there.
Historic summer and a restless world launched
in borrowed kit, like a chaotic jumble sale of purpose
when pioneers came out of shadows imposed by others.
As the rust-bucket engines of misogyny billowed guff
and the double breasted growlers of ignorance schemed,
Elsie Cook stitched her national pride on to emboldened
jerseys for her team to kick their defiant ball into relevance

but this wasn't queuing around the stadium relevance or the
sway and surge of 70's dodgy fashion in a tapestry of booze
gargled abuse relevance or intimate examinations of a referee's
lineage. This was relevance of innocent effort to fix injustice.

An eternity where women had been sidelined from a game
they'd long played, in and around the dead of ancient kirkyards
and the cobblestone factory courts of jute spun empires – banned
yet the spirit of playing the game for the sake of it burned deep.

For a moment, imagine being told you couldn't play football
like those diamonds of steely graft. Sisters of the Undiscovered
that noble afternoon with shoulders braced against the wall
tagged with 'stick tae bingo – fitba's no fer wee lassies'.

Aye right! So it's no! And so the frost bound clatter of battle
punched a hole through feeble attempts to hold back their
escape into the normality of everyone pitchside and beyond
the dreich stadium to splinter into a million arguments about
          nothing.

Janie Houghton, Jane Hunter, June Hunter, Linda Kidd,
   Sandra Walker,
Mary Carr, Marion Mount, Rose Reilly, Edna Neillis,
   Mary Anderson,
Margaret McAulay, Angela Creamer, Mary Davenport,
   Linda Cooper,
Diane McClaren, Irene Morrison and oh aye, of course Elsie Cook.

Stand proud Ravenscraig Pioneers. Accept praise and respect establishing yourselves in the pantheon of sporting greats yet with humble dignity mixed with passion for that ordinary thing we call the beautiful game which can, and now, is played by
   anyone.

IN THEIR OWN WORDS
Collected by Karen Fraser

MARGARET MCAULAY: *Debut for the Scottish Women's Football Team in 1972 at the first ever international against England. Appearances: 23.*

The first International was on 18 November 1972. It was a freezing cold day, don't know if that was the first or second goal I scored. I ended up tearing a ligament behind my knee, and I couldnae because it was so cold, I couldnae play on, had to go off. It was Saturday, 18 November 1972. One of the match reports said, 'for 4-2-4 read 36-24-36' – the first International in 1972 and they are talking like that – *Sunday Post* it was.

I played for Westthorn United and I remember playing with Rose Reilly and Edna Neillis – they moved to the team as it became more successful. There was also Mary Carr and Mary Anderson and we all ended up playing in the same international team – we were obviously a very successful football team.

Sometimes you only played one international match a year or if you got a tournament obviously you were playing in the tournament against other teams but sometimes just one a year. Which is why I only played 23 times over like a big span you know from 1972 to 1981 but I only played 23 times because that was all the internationals we had.

We did play in Italy, at the San Siro, [in Milan]. We were definitely there twice because I have two medals, we obviously played several matches in the tournaments, we definitely played France and Denmark.

One game that stands out is the day we beat England – the one and only time in 1977. We beat them in Dundee and it's never been done since. That sticks out because again it was a one-off and at the time, I didn't think it was going to be all those years and still never, you know, that will be 40, 42 year ago.

By playing an international you were putting down a

statement about the women's game in Scotland. Northern Ireland, Republic of Ireland, Wales they all wanted to come and play against us.

The high was winning with Scotland against England (1977) and being the captain of the first Scotland team [in 1972] was pretty special, especially as I never expected it. Being the first one, selected by Rab, and he didnae know me from anybody in the team when he came in. It was totally unexpected by me, I am no one of these people who think they are the greatest thing in the world. If you get to that stage you give up because you are always learning. It was totally unexpected and what bigger honour can you get than to be in the first international and to be captain as well and that is going to stand for ever, they cannot change it. I got a nice write-up in the programme, what he thought of me, which again was totally unexpected.

SHEILA BEGBIE: *Debut for Scottish Women's Football Team in 1973. Captained the team on several occasions including the 1977 2–1 win over England. Appearances: 25.*

I went along to Edinburgh Dynamos and I got into the team straight away, I was about thirteen and played every week. At that point, I would be playing against women who were 30, 35 years old. I think I was probably quite mature in terms of my years and my age. So straight into the main team – there was only one team so it's not like they had a youth section! So, into the women's team and I got my first international cap at fifteen, still a child technically.

I did not play in the first international which was at Ravenscraig against England, but the next international, I did. I think it came through the club, through my coach who said to me, 'Oh, by the way, you've been asked to go training with the Scotland team at the weekend'. Which was great and actually I found recently a note I had from the guy who was the Scotland coach at that point, his name was Angus Williamson. In a little brown envelope, just a little slip of paper, saying, 'You've been selected to play for Scotland and be the Captain too, please'. I would have been about eighteen or nineteen at this point, something like that.

Edinburgh Dynamos were amazing – I think at one point we had something like nine players in the national team, we were the spine of the Scotland team. I loved playing for the National team.

JANE LEGGETT: *Debut for the Scottish Women's Football Team in 1976. Appearances: 29.*

The Scotland team started in 1972 and I had gone along to watch the game. It was the aim of players to push themselves to get into the Scotland team, especially players from Edinburgh Dynamos, Westthorn United and Dundee. Anyone who was a half-decent player wanted to be doing that. Unfortunately, there were not a lot of international matches, they were few and far between in those days.

There were a couple of girls from the Edinburgh Dynamos team who played for Scotland – Maggie Wilson and Shelia Begbie – so they were the first two from the team and that was an incentive. If people from our team are getting recognised then hopefully one day you will get recognised yourself. I trained hard and played as well as I could and then I managed to play for Scotland but did not get picked again for a while and I thought I need to get back in that squad. Eventually I did and I thought '*I have to use this opportunity*', so before I left Edinburgh in the 1980s, I was training Monday to Friday in the evening and sometimes on a Saturday to play on a Sunday. I was also playing for Scotland and so it was important to make sure that my fitness levels were right. I used to train up at Meadowbank including weight training. By then I was playing for a team called Inveralmond and they trained once a week in Livingston and we were a good team which helped me play for Scotland.

I was aware of the lack of press coverage. I think the biggest shock I had was when I went to Italy and realised how big football was there and how supportive they were. Teams would be playing at decent stadiums and you could lift a newspaper and there would be a decent article about a women's game. It was like another world, so advanced. I could not believe that many people had turned up to watch a game. You would have an international in Scotland and maybe 50 to 100 people would watch, go to Italy and there were thousands, it was just another world. Here I would reckon that it was not until sometime in the 1980s when the women's game started to get better press coverage but still not enough to hit you in the face.

THE CHALLENGES OF (RE)WRITING WOMEN'S FOOTBALL HISTORY

Andrew Mitchell

HOW MANY CAPS have you got? If you played for Scotland, you ought to know the answer – but if you are a woman whose playing days ended a few years ago, you might struggle to establish even the most basic facts of your career, far less how many internationals you played.

The rare honour of playing for Scotland deserves to be recognised, as anyone who witnessed the emotionally-charged presentation of retrospective caps before Scotland played England in 2023 will understand.

Yet finding those women who came to Hampden, and confirming they actually represented their country, was no easy task. Unearthing fundamental facts like who played and when, which are vital to prove the eligibility of individuals for a cap, could be like banging your head against a brick wall.

That's because the pursuit of historical accuracy – every match, every player, every goal – is fraught with serious obstacles, not just because many details have been lost in the mists of time, but also because the facts themselves can sometimes get in the way of a good story.

The memory can play tricks, as I found when speaking to former players. For example, I had a terse exchange with one internationalist when I told her she had played 37 times for Scotland. She came straight back to assert that she had 48 caps, and even when I presented her with a list of matches, nothing I could say would make her believe any different. She was rightly proud of her contribution to the national team and no mere statistician was going to 'rob' her of 11 caps.

Another Scotland player was adamant she had scored at the San Siro against Italy, and she had indeed played in the famous Milan arena in 1974, but Scotland didn't find the net in that particular game and lost by three goals to nil. In fact, her strike came four years later in the rather less glamorous Stadio Adriatico in Pescara, confirmed in an Italian newspaper archive which described her '*splendida rete su calcio piazzato*' ('a fine goal from a free kick').

Make no mistake, researching the history of the Scotland women's team is a challenge, and it goes far beyond caps and goals: until very recently, amazingly enough, there was no definitive list of Scotland internationals. There were many question marks over games, dates, venues and results.

Starting out with only the most basic information, the first fundamental step was to work out which matches were played. This was easier said than done, as by the time the Scottish FA took over the women's team in the autumn of 1997, there were precious few records left from the first 25 years of internationals. Any documents kept by the Scottish Women's FA were passed from secretary to secretary over the years, and most ended up being lost along the way.

As for media coverage, it was minimal because the all-male football fraternity refused to take the women's game seriously. While a few internationals got a good spread in the papers, the majority did not and some seem to have escaped the press entirely. For example, Scotland faced Denmark in a friendly in 1986 at an almost deserted Meadowbank Stadium on a Saturday evening, after Meadowbank Thistle played Stenhousemuir in a league game that afternoon. It was too late for that night's sports papers, and only the briefest of mentions in the *Edinburgh Evening News* a few days later confirmed it had gone ahead; no match report was published anywhere and the Scotland line-up remains unknown.

The remedy was to be relentless in tracking down details, whether in local papers, in personal archives (some players kept scrapbooks, bless them!) or scribbled notes in match programmes. I even became a dab hand at tracking down middle-aged former players on Facebook to ask them what they remembered of their playing careers.

In time, after a lot of digging and crosschecking, a tentative list of matches, venues and results was compiled, but it still needed confirmation from the Scottish FA as to which games should be classified as full internationals. This is an issue which the national body has struggled with over the years: for example, Scotland's men have been awarded caps for matches which should really have no place in the records, against a West Norwegian Select (1929), Canada Amateurs (1967) and the Hong Kong League (2002).

For the women's team, every game had to be assessed for approval. Decisions had to be made to exclude games where the Scotland team was fully representative but the opposition was not a *bona fide* national team, for example Sardinia (1981), Grand Hotel Varna (1992) and Isle of Man (2000), not to mention USA Under 18s (2000) and Sweden Under 21s (2001). On top of that, there were closed-door internationals, exhibition matches, tour games and more.

Most of these could be discounted easily enough, but some subtle nuances and discrepancies could cause confusion and disagreement. Notably, what should we make of Scotland's game against England at Wembley in May 1990? Two full-strength sides entertained the crowd before the FA Cup final, and England won 4–0 but the game was played just twenty minutes each way. It hardly meets the definition of a 'full' international yet the Football Association decided it did, while the Scottish FA has taken the opposite view.

After all that, the upshot is that precisely 81 internationals which took place under the Scottish Women's FA between 1972 and 1997 have now been accepted and verified by the Scottish FA.

The next step was to work out who actually played in these games and would therefore be eligible to receive a cap. Despite the combined efforts of myself and a small number of other historians, in particular Elsie Cook, Karen Fraser, Fiona Skillen and Neil Morrison, it is a process that is still underway and may never be completed because there is so little in the way of detailed contemporary reports.

To make things worse, although digitisation has revolutionised the number of resources available, not all the published records that do exist can be taken for granted.

Even UEFA cannot be considered a definitive source, as you will find when you check their official record of qualifiers in the European Championship.

There are discrepancies between their 'official' stats and other accounts, with one example being the Netherlands vs Scotland game in 1987. According to UEFA, Scotland's second substitute was Mandy Doogan, coming on for Pauline Brown after 70 minutes; the trouble is, Mandy was a goalkeeper and hardly likely to replace an outfield player. I spoke to Shelley Valle (who UEFA said was an unused sub), and she recalled with clarity coming on against the Dutch to make her international debut.

Frustratingly, UEFA's match stats in the 1980s also frequently lack details such as scorers, attendance and team captain.

Even after the Scottish FA took over the women's team in 1997, they could let matters slip in a way that would be unthinkable for the men's game. I have inside knowledge of this: I was a press officer at the Scottish FA when Julie Fleeting was coming up for her 100th cap, a terrific achievement that was going to be celebrated with a presentation before the record-breaking match.

I was not convinced that the total was correct (although at that time I could not prove it) and raised my concerns, only to be told brusquely to 'back off'. The ceremony went ahead with widespread media coverage and only now, having laboriously established her full match record, can it be said for certain that the presentation actually took place on the occasion of her 96th Scotland cap. Oops.

What is more, when Julie ended her international career,

with an MBE after her name, she was universally credited with 116 goals in 121 games – but she actually scored 110 goals in 118 internationals.

The issue is not confined to Julie as several others in the Scottish FA Roll of Honour have demonstrably false cap totals. This is no fault of the players, but an example of 'guesstimates' becoming accepted because there was no firm evidence to the contrary. Gradually, as evidence mounts up, these errors are being corrected.

This 'fake history' is not a new trend in women's football, nor is it confined to Scotland. The scourge of misreporting has been prevalent since the dawn of the game in the Victorian era, when the very first organised matches in 1881 were featured in the newspapers more for their capacity for scandal than as serious football.

This has led to all sorts of myths and mistruths being circulated about the early players, and is particularly prevalent in relation to the British Ladies' Football Club founded in 1895, whose story has only really started to interest historians in the current century.

By the time Nettie Honeyball and her fellow players took the field, there was a slightly improved attitude in the press to the concept of women playing football, which meant that the sceptical and mocking reports were sometimes balanced by others which took a genuine interest in their exploits.

Nevertheless, the overall lack of a detailed record has left modern historians with a lot of catching up to do and sent them down a few blind alleys. Some frankly dodgy research has led to mistaken conclusions about the players being published and once these things get on Wikipedia they are very hard to shift – the most extreme example being on Emma Clarke of the British Ladies' Football Club whose entire Wiki page is about the wrong person.

While the Victorian era might be expected to present a

challenge to researchers, the modern era fares little better. One relatively topical example is the story of legendary Scotland internationalist Rose Reilly winning the World Cup with Italy. This is now acknowledged to be a romantic fiction, as the 1984 'Mundialito' was really a four-team invitational tournament, with all the participants coming from Europe. Tellingly, England won the next edition of the 'Mundialito' but don't claim to be World Cup winners, nor does anyone suggest that Scotland reached a World Cup final in 1978 when Italy hosted a six-team tournament, also described as a 'Mundialito'.

I could offer many other examples, but the message is clear. There is a desperate need for more detailed research into the history of women's football and its players. Little is lost and much is gained by unearthing the truth, as the women's stories are so inspirational and interesting even without the myths and the mistakes.

The digitisation of newspapers and other archives has helped to fill in many of the gaps, but the search for clues is a massive jigsaw puzzle and while much progress has been made there is a long way to go.

Thankfully several players kept scrapbooks of newspaper cuttings and memorabilia, and some have even donated their collections to the Scottish Football Museum, notably Margaret McAulay and Jane Legget. Others have dug deep into their memories, and one thing I have learned from speaking to players is that they almost always remember their first international cap. That's because playing for Scotland is life-defining, and as most of them were barely allowed to celebrate the achievement at the time, it reinforces the need to give them official recognition now.

It makes historians like me all the more determined to ensure the women's national team is properly recorded. I hope that one day, every woman who has pulled on a Scotland shirt to represent her country can proudly show off her commemorative cap and point to her name in the national team archive.

SCOTLAND'S INTERNATIONAL MATCH RECORD IN FULL

	Date	Opposition	For/Against	
1	18–Nov–72	England	2	3
2	23–Jun–73	England	0	8
3	21–Sep–74	Italy	3	4
4	24–Sep–74	Italy	0	3
5	23–Nov–74	Northern Ireland	11	1
6	26–Apr–75	Wales	3	2
7	18–Apr–76	Republic of Ireland	3	3
8	21–May–76	Wales	3	2
9	23–May–76	England	1	5
10	04–Jul–76	Republic of Ireland	3	1
11	26–Sep–76	Wales	2	2
12	29–May–77	England	2	1
13	29–Oct–77	Northern Ireland	4	1
14	28–May–78	Northern Ireland	2	1
15	29–Jul–78	Switzerland	0	0
16	31–Jul–78	Yugoslavia	3	2
17	05–Aug–78	Italy	1	4
18	22–Apr–79	Wales	2	0
19	02–Jun–79	Northern Ireland	3	0
20	20–Jul–79	France	0	0
21	22–Jul–79	Denmark	0	2
22	27–Apr–80	Wales	1	0
23	29–Mar–81	Republic of Ireland	5	0
24	26–Apr–81	Wales	0	0
25	22–Aug–81	Italy	0	3
26	25–Aug–81	Belgium	1	0
27	20–Sep–81	Iceland	3	2
28	19–Aug–82	Italy	2	1
29	22–Aug–82	Italy	1	4

Stadium

Ravenscraig Stadium, Greenock
Manor Park, Nuneaton
Stadio Bruno Benelli, Ravenna
San Siro, Milan
Kilbowie Park, Clydebank
Douglas Park, Hamilton
Dalymount Park, Dublin
Woodside Stadium, Watford
Southbury Road, Enfield
Grangemouth Stadium

Jenner Park, Barry
Downfield Park, Dundee
Inver Park, Larne
Warout Stadium, Glenrothes
Stadio Comunale, Atri
Stadio Comunale, Atri
Stadio Adriatico, Pescara
Downfield Park, Dundee
Dixon Park, Ballyclare
Stadio Comunale, Rimini

Stadio Comunale, Riccione
Cwmbran Stadium, Cwmbran
Dalymount Park, Dublin
Douglas Park, Hamilton
Stadio Mariotti, Alghero
Stadio Comunale, Sennori
Boghead Park, Dumbarton
Stadio Comunale, Monfalcone
Campo Sportivo, Grado

30	04–Sep–82	Northern Ireland	2	1
31	19–Sep–82	Republic of Ireland	3	0
32	03–Oct–82	England	0	4
33	13–Mar–83	Republic of Ireland	1	1
34	17–Apr–83	Northern Ireland	3	0
35	22–May–83	England	0	2
36	22–Apr–84	Wales	1	1
37	27–May–84	Republic of Ireland	0	1
38	17–Mar–85	England	0	4
39	02–Jun–85	Republic of Ireland	2	1
40	23–Nov–85	Northern Ireland	9	1
41	03–May–86	Denmark	0	1
42	25–May–86	Northern Ireland	7	0
43	28–Sep–86	Republic of Ireland	5	1
44	12–Oct–86	England	1	3
45	07–Nov–87	Netherlands	0	4
46	03–Apr–88	Republic of Ireland	1	2
47	30–Apr–89	England	0	3
48	21–Apr–90	Northern Ireland	4	1
49	06–May–90	England	0	4
50	20–Apr–91	England	0	5
51	31–Mar–92	North Korea	0	1
52	03–Apr–92	Bulgaria	3	0
53	05–Apr–92	CIS (Russia)	2	1
54	18–Apr–92	England	0	1
55	20–May–92	Iceland	0	0
56	22–Jun–92	Iceland	1	2
57	23–Aug–92	England	0	2
58	16–Oct–93	Italy	0	4
59	26–Feb–94	France	0	1
60	03–Apr–94	Italy	0	4
61	24–Apr–94	Portugal	1	2

Seaview, Belfast

East End Park, Dunfermline
Boghead Park, Dumbarton
Dalymount Park, Dublin
Petershill Stadium, Glasgow
Elland Road, Leeds
Eirias Park, Colwyn Bay
Station Park, Baillieston
Deepdale, Preston
Tinto Park, Glasgow
Junior National Stadium, Belfast

Meadowbank Stadium, Edinburgh
Boghead Park, Dumbarton
Tolka Park, Dublin
Stark's Park, Kirkcaldy
Sportpark De Kollenberg, Nuth
Frank Cooke Park, Dublin
Stark's Park, Kirkcaldy
Stair Park, Stranraer
St Mirren Park, Paisley
Adams Park, Wycombe

Varna Stadium, Varna
Varna Stadium, Varna
Varna Stadium, Varna
Bescot Stadium, Walsall
McDiarmid Park, Perth
Akranesvöllur, Akranes
McDiarmid Park, Perth
Stadio Comunale, Senigallia
Stade Municipale, Ozoir-la-Ferrière
Forthbank Stadium, Stirling

Forthbank Stadium, Stirling

62	09–May–94	Iceland	1	4
63	29–May–94	Portugal	2	8
64	25–Sep–94	France	0	3
65	17–May–95	Australia	0	0
66	23–Oct–95	Faroe Islands	7	1
67	05–Nov–95	Republic of Ireland	0	2
68	26–Nov–95	Belgium	0	3
69	24–Mar–96	Wales	1	5
70	07–Apr–96	Republic of Ireland	2	1
71	20–Apr–96	Belgium	1	6
72	25–May–96	Faroe Islands	3	0
73	02–Jun–96	Wales	3	2
74	17–Nov–96	Wales	0	2
75	10–Dec–96	Brazil	0	5
76	12–Dec–96	Brazil	0	6
77	14–Dec–96	Brazil	1	7
78	09–Mar–97	England	0	6
79	23–Aug–97	England	0	4
80	03–Sep–97	Estonia	7	1
81	07–Sep–97	Lithuania	5	0
82	26–Apr–98	Czech Republic	1	1
83	03–May–98	Estonia	7	0
84	23–May–98	Czech Republic	1	1
85	31–May–98	Lithuania	17	0
86	13–Sep–98	Spain	0	3
87	11–Oct–98	Spain	1	4
88	16–Dec–98	Netherlands	0	1
89	13–Apr–99	Romania	3	3
90	14–Apr–99	Moldova	5	0
91	15–Apr–99	Russia	0	0
92	17–Apr–99	North Korea	1	1
93	18–Apr–99	Russia	0	3
94	09–May–99	France	3	4

Tinto Park, Glasgow
Estádio de Mello, Almeirim
Allan Park, Aberdeen
Rugby Park, Kilmarnock
Palmerston Park, Dumfries
Tolka Park, Dublin
St Mirren Park, Paisley
Latham Park, Newtown
Forthbank Stadium, Stirling

Stade Communal, Namur
Leikvöllur, Toftir
Allan Park, Aberdeen
Somerset Park, Ayr
Parque Sao Jorge, Sao Paulo
Estádio Novelli Júnior, Itu
Estádio Dr Jayme Cintra, Jundiaí
Bramall Lane, Sheffield
Almondvale Stadium, Livingston
Maarjamäe Stadium, Tallinn

Zalgiris Stadium, Vilnius
Podjestedsky Stadium, Cesky Dub
Somerset Park, Ayr
Caledonian Stadium, Inverness
Scotstoun Stadium, Glasgow
Forthbank Stadium, Stirling
El Fontanar Stadium, Cordoba
Sportpark Saestum, Zeist
Varna Stadium, Varna
Varna Stadium, Varna

Varna Stadium, Varna
Varna Stadium, Varna
Varna Stadium, Varna
Excelsior Stadium, Airdrie

95	14–Aug–99	Finland	0	2
96	03–Oct–99	Republic of Ireland	3	0
97	23–Oct–99	Croatia	3	4
98	14–Nov–99	Czech Republic	2	1
99	26–Feb–00	France	2	1
100	02–Apr–00	Moldova	5	0
101	03–Apr–00	Ukraine	3	3
102	05–Apr–00	Romania	2	0
103	29–Apr–00	Republic of Ireland	3	0
104	14–May–00	Croatia	4	1
105	11–Aug–00	Netherlands	2	3
106	13–Aug–00	Belgium	3	4
107	26–Aug–00	Czech Republic	1	5
108	18–Sep–00	Netherlands	1	3
109	19–Sep–00	Belarus	2	2
110	22–Sep–00	Republic of Ireland	0	1
111	29–Nov–00	Northern Ireland	9	0
112	17–Jan–01	Italy	0	3
113	17–Feb–01	Portugal	2	2
114	17–Mar–01	France	0	5
115	10–May–01	Netherlands	0	2
116	27–May–01	England	0	1
117	11–Aug–01	Republic of Ireland	2	1
118	12–Aug–01	Republic of Ireland	1	4
119	29–Sep–01	Austria	2	1
120	28–Oct–01	Wales	3	0
121	25–Nov–01	Belgium	2	3
122	01–Mar–02	Canada	0	3
123	03–Mar–02	Portugal	2	1
124	05–Mar–02	Wales	1	0
125	07–Mar–02	England	1	4
126	21–Apr–02	Belgium	4	0
127	05–May–02	Austria	5	0

Kauniaisten Centre, Kauniainen
Broadwood Stadium, Cumbernauld
Stadion Veli Joze, Poreč
Broadwood Stadium, Cumbernauld
Stade Patrice Brocas, Auch
Obrochiste Stadium, Albena

Obrochiste Stadium, Albena
Obrochiste Stadium, Albena
Richmond Park, Dublin
Forthbank Stadium, Stirling
Sportpark Berestein, Hilversum
Stadium Internos, Etten-Leur
FK Chmel Stadium, Blšany
Sportpark Panhuis, Veenendaal
Sportpark Panhuis, Veenendaal
Lough Moss Centre, Carryduff

Keswick Athletic Centre, Dumfries
Luigi Razza Stadium, Vibo Valentia
Estádio Municipal 25 de Abril, Castro Verde
Stade de Penvillers, Quimper
Almondvale Stadium, Livingston
Reebok Stadium, Bolton
Clonshaugh, Dublin
Clonshaugh, Dublin
Waldstadion, Leopoldsdorf
Almondvale Stadium, Livingston

Puyenbeke, Sint-Niklaas
Estádio Municipal, Quarteira
Estádio Municipal, Lagoa
Estádio Dr Francisco Vieira, Silves
Estádio Municipal, Quarteira
Almondvale Stadium, Livingston
Almondvale Stadium, Livingston

128	19–May–02	Wales	2	0
129	08–Sep–02	USA	2	8
130	15–Dec–02	Netherlands	0	0
131	18–Dec–02	Portugal	2	0
132	22–Jan–03	Italy	1	4
133	10–Mar–03	China	0	1
134	27–Mar–03	Germany	0	5
135	01–May–03	Belgium	0	0
136	18–May–03	Ukraine	5	1
137	07–Jun–03	Portugal	8	1
138	12–Aug–03	Greece	2	0
139	06–Sep–03	Australia	0	1
140	09–Sep–03	Italy	0	4
141	01–Oct–03	Netherlands	0	2
142	19–Oct–03	Czech Republic	0	2
143	13–Nov–03	England	0	5
144	15–Jan–04	Greece	1	1
145	17–Jan–04	Greece	3	0
146	18–Feb–04	France	1	1
147	21–Feb–04	France	3	6
148	10–Mar–04	Iceland	1	5
149	10–Apr–04	Ukraine	0	1
150	02–May–04	Germany	1	3
151	23–May–04	Portugal	2	1
152	19–Aug–04	Switzerland	6	0
153	05–Sep–04	Czech Republic	3	2
154	21–Apr–05	England	1	2
155	20–May–05	Finland	0	2
156	25–May–05	Iceland	0	2
157	31–Jul–05	Northern Ireland	2	1
158	28–Aug–05	Russia	0	6
159	25–Sep–05	Republic of Ireland	0	0
160	13–Oct–05	Germany	0	4

Penydarren Park, Merthyr Tydfil
Columbus Crew Stadium, Ohio
Praia da Falésia, Albufeira

Estádio Capitão Josino da Costa, Lagoa
Stadio Flaminio, Rome
Almondvale Stadium, Livingston
Karl-Leibknecht Stadium, Potsdam
Almondvale Stadium, Livingston
Almondvale Stadium, Livingston
Estádio Municipal, Nelas
Prosfyghika Stadium, Patras
Almondvale Stadium, Livingston
Almondvale Stadium, Livingston

Almondvale Stadium, Livingston
Stadion SK Kravaře Stadium, Kravaře
Deepdale, Preston
Athletic Centre, Agios Kosmas
Athletic Centre, Agios Kosmas
Stade Louis-Michel, Sète
Stade Louis Mosson, Montpellier
Egilshöll, Reykjavik
Lokomotiv Stadium, Simferopol
Almondvale Stadium, Livingston

Almondvale Stadium, Livingston
Victoria Park, Dingwall
Victoria Park, Dingwall
Prenton Park, Birkenhead
Veritas Stadium, Turku
McDiarmid Park, Perth
McDiarmid Park, Perth
Moskvich Stadium, Moscow
McDiarmid Park, Perth
HW Wild Stadium, Bayreuth

161	08–Mar–06	Italy	0	4
162	10–Mar–06	Japan	0	4
163	26–Apr–06	Switzerland	1	0
164	06–May–06	Republic of Ireland	2	0
165	24–May–06	Russia	0	4
166	03–Aug–06	Finland	0	0
167	26–Aug–06	Switzerland	1	1
168	06–Sep–06	Belgium	3	0
169	23–Sep–06	Germany	0	5
170	14–Feb–07	Japan	0	2
171	17–Feb–07	Sweden	0	1
172	11–Mar–07	England	0	1
173	06–Apr–07	Italy	2	1
174	06–May–07	Portugal	0	0
175	30–May–07	Ukraine	1	2
176	26–Aug–07	Belgium	3	2
177	26–Sep–07	Finland	0	1
178	29–Sep–07	Finland	1	4
179	27–Oct–07	Slovakia	3	0
180	31–Oct–07	Denmark	0	1
181	05–Mar–08	USA Under 20s	1	2
182	07–Mar–08	Netherlands	0	1
183	10–Mar–08	Canada	2	0
184	12–Mar–08	Russia	2	3
185	09–Apr–08	Belgium	1	0
186	27–Apr–08	Denmark	1	2
187	03–May–08	Portugal	4	1
188	28–May–08	Ukraine	0	1
189	24–Aug–08	Finland	0	3
190	27–Aug–08	Finland	1	1
191	17–Sep–08	Switzerland	4	0
192	28–Sep–08	Slovakia	6	0
193	26–Oct–08	Russia	2	3

Stadio Le Piane, Isernia
Stadio Civitelle, Agnone
McDiarmid Park, Perth
Richmond Park, Dublin
McDiarmid Park, Perth
McDiarmid Park, Perth
Sportzentrum Schlossfeld, Willisau
RJ Wavre Stadium, Wavre
McDiarmid Park, Perth
Dasaki Stadium, Achna

Ammochostos Stadium, Larnaca
Adams Park, Wycombe
McDiarmid Park, Perth
McDiarmid Park, Perth
Illichivets Stadium, Mariupol
McDiarmid Park, Perth
Veritas Stadium, Turku
Olympic Stadium, Helsinki
NTC Senec, Senec
McDiarmid Park, Perth

Paralimni Stadium, Paralimni
Paralimni Stadium, Paralimni
Alpha Sports Centre, Larnaca
GSP Stadium, Nicosia
Bergestadion, Tienen
Viborg Stadium, Viborg
Estádio Municipal, Póvoa de Varzim
McDiarmid Park, Perth
Pietarsaaren, Jakobstad
Hietalahti Stadium, Vaasa

McDiarmid Park, Perth
McDiarmid Park, Perth
Tynecastle Park, Edinburgh

194	30–Oct–08	Russia	2	1
195	05–Mar–09	France	0	2
196	07–Mar–09	South Africa	0	2
197	10–Mar–09	England	0	3
198	12–Mar–09	Russia	2	1
199	08–Apr–09	Italy	1	4
200	12–May–09	Northern Ireland	3	1
201	12–Aug–09	France	0	4
202	14–Aug–09	Denmark	2	5
203	09–Sep–09	Switzerland	0	0
204	15–Oct–09	Northern Ireland	3	0
205	24–Oct–09	Greece	1	0
206	29–Oct–09	Georgia	3	1
207	24–Feb–10	Netherlands	1	4
208	26–Feb–10	Italy	0	2
209	01–Mar–10	New Zealand	0	3
210	03–Mar–10	South Africa	2	1
211	27–Mar–10	Georgia	3	1
212	01–Apr–10	Bulgaria	8	1
213	23–May–10	Northern Ireland	2	0
214	05–Jun–10	Switzerland	3	3
215	08–Jun–10	Switzerland	1	0
216	19–Jun–10	Bulgaria	5	0
217	24–Jun–10	Denmark	0	1
218	23–Jul–10	Poland	2	1
219	21–Aug–10	Greece	4	1
220	25–Aug–10	Denmark	0	0
221	13–Feb–11	Wales	4	2
222	02–Mar–11	Canada	0	1
223	04–Mar–11	England	2	0
224	07–Mar–11	Italy	0	0
225	09–Mar–11	France	0	3
226	03–Apr–11	Netherlands	2	6

Spartak Stadium, Nalchik
Ammochostos Stadium, Larnaca
GSP Stadium, Nicosia
GSZ Stadium, Larnaca
GSP Stadium, Nicosia
Rugby Park, Kilmarnock
Forthbank Stadium, Stirling

Stade des Grands Pres, Chartres
Gladsaxe Stadium, Søborg
GC Campus, Niederhasli
The Oval, Belfast
Pathiakakis Stadium, Ano Liosia
Tynecastle Park, Edinburgh
GSP Stadium, Nicosia
GSZ Stadium, Larnaca
GSZ Stadium, Larnaca
GSZ Stadium, Larnaca

Meskhi Stadium, Tbilisi
Falkirk Stadium, Falkirk
Strathclyde Homes Stadium, Dumbarton
Stadion Niedermatten, Wohlen
Herti Allmend Stadion, Zug
Asparuhov Stadium, Sofia
Rugby Park, Kilmarnock
Stadion Miejski, Proszowice
Strathclyde Homes Stadium, Dumbarton
Vejle Stadium, Vejle

Bridge Meadow, Haverfordwest
Ammochostos Stadium, Larnaca
GSP Stadium, Nicosia
GSZ Stadium, Larnaca
GSP Stadium, Nicosia
Kras Stadion, Volendam

227	18–May–11	France	1	1
228	21–Aug–11	Switzerland	5	0
229	23–Aug–11	Belgium	1	0
230	18–Sep–11	Finland	0	1
231	21–Sep–11	Finland	7	2
232	12–Oct–11	Israel	6	1
233	27–Oct–11	Wales	2	2
234	05–Feb–12	Northern Ireland	5	1
235	28–Feb–12	Canada	1	5
236	01–Mar–12	Netherlands	2	1
237	04–Mar–12	Italy	1	2
238	06–Mar–12	South Africa	2	0
239	31–Mar–12	France	0	2
240	05–Apr–12	Republic of Ireland	2	1
241	09–May–12	Poland	3	1
242	26–May–12	Sweden	1	4
243	16–Jun–12	Israel	8	0
244	21–Jun–12	Republic of Ireland	1	0
245	15–Jul–12	Cameroon	2	0
246	04–Aug–12	Iceland	1	1
247	30–Aug–12	Norway	2	2
248	15–Sep–12	Wales	2	1
249	19–Sep–12	France	0	5
250	20–Oct–12	Spain	1	1
251	24–Oct–12	Spain	2	3
252	09–Feb–13	USA	1	4
253	14–Feb–13	USA	1	3
254	06–Mar–13	New Zealand	0	1
255	08–Mar–13	England	4	4
256	11–Mar–13	Italy	2	1
257	13–Mar–13	Netherlands	1	0
258	07–Apr–13	Wales	2	1
259	01–Jun–13	Iceland	3	2

Stade Francis-le-Blé, Brest
Falkirk Stadium, Falkirk
Falkirk Stadium, Falkirk
Sonera Stadium, Helsinki

Tynecastle Park, Edinburgh
Ness Ziona Stadium, Ness Ziona
Tynecastle Park, Edinburgh
Solitude, Belfast
GSZ Stadium, Larnaca
GSP Stadium, Nicosia
GSZ Stadium, Larnaca
Paralimni Stadium, Paralimni
Stade Jules-Deschaseaux, Le Havre
Tynecastle Park, Edinburgh

Stadion Kazimierz Deyna, Gdansk
Stark's Park, Kirkcaldy
Tynecastle Park, Edinburgh
Turners Cross, Cork
Chris Anderson Stadium, Aberdeen
Cappielow Park, Greenock
East End Park, Dunfermline
Parc y Scarlets, Llanelli
Tynecastle Park, Edinburgh
Hampden Park, Glasgow

Ciudad del Fútbol, Las Rozas
EverBank Field, Jacksonville
LP Field, Nashville
GSP Stadium, Nicosia
GSZ Stadium, Larnaca
GSZ Stadium, Larnaca
GSP Stadium, Nicosia
East End Park, Dunfermline
Laugardalsvöllur, Reykjavik

260	15–Jun–13	Germany	0	3
261	21–Aug–13	Serbia	1	1
262	22–Sep–13	Faroe Islands	7	2
263	26–Sep–13	Bosnia Herzegovina	7	0
264	26–Oct–13	Northern Ireland	2	0
265	31–Oct–13	Poland	4	0
266	12–Dec–13	Canada	0	2
267	15–Dec–13	Brazil	1	3
268	18–Dec–13	Chile	3	4
269	22–Dec–13	Canada	0	1
270	13–Feb–14	Finland	1	3
271	05–Mar–14	France	1	1
272	07–Mar–14	Netherlands	4	3
273	10–Mar–14	Australia	4	2
274	12–Mar–14	South Korea	1	1
275	05–Apr–14	Poland	2	0
276	10–Apr–14	Bosnia Herzegovina	3	1
277	14–Jun–14	Sweden	1	3
278	19–Jun–14	Northern Ireland	2	0
279	03–Aug–14	Wales	1	1
280	20–Aug–14	Portugal	1	1
281	13–Sep–14	Faroe Islands	9	0
282	17–Sep–14	Sweden	0	2
283	25–Oct–14	Netherlands	1	2
284	30–Oct–14	Netherlands	0	2
285	08–Feb–15	Northern Ireland	4	0
286	04–Mar–15	Canada	0	2
287	06–Mar–15	Italy	2	3
288	09–Mar–15	South Korea	2	1
289	11–Mar–15	Netherlands	3	1
290	09–Apr–15	Australia	1	1
291	28–May–15	France	0	1

Stadion Essen, Essen

Sports Centre, Stara Pazova
Tórsvøllur, Torshavn
Fir Park, Motherwell
Fir Park, Motherwell
Grodzisk Wielkopolski
Estádio Nacional, Brasilia
Estádio Nacional, Brasilia
Estádio Nacional, Brasilia
Estádio Nacional, Brasilia
Eerikkilä Sport Resort, Tammela

GSZ Stadium, Larnaca
GSP Stadium, Nicosia
GSZ Stadium, Larnaca
GSZ Stadium, Larnaca
Fir Park, Motherwell
Bilino Polje, Zenica
Fir Park, Motherwell
Solitude, Belfast
Palmerston Park, Dumfries
Estádio Dr Matos, Viana do Castelo

Fir Park, Motherwell
Ullevi, Gothenburg
Tynecastle Park, Edinburgh
Sparta Stadium, Rotterdam
Solitude, Belfast
GSP Stadium, Nicosia
GSZ Stadium, Larnaca
GSZ Stadium, Larnaca
Ammochostos Stadium, Larnaca
Falkirk Stadium, Falkirk

Stade Marcel Picot, Nancy

292	17–Sep–15	Norway	0	4
293	22–Sep–15	Slovenia	3	0
294	23–Oct–15	Belarus	7	0
295	27–Oct–15	Macedonia	4	1
296	29–Nov–15	Macedonia	10	0
297	26–Jan–16	Sweden	0	6
298	08–Mar–16	Spain	1	1
299	08–Apr–16	Slovenia	3	1
300	03–Jun–16	Iceland	0	4
301	07–Jun–16	Belarus	1	0
302	20–Sep–16	Iceland	2	1
303	20–Oct–16	Netherlands	0	7
304	20–Jan–17	Denmark	2	2
305	23–Jan–17	Denmark	1	1
306	01–Mar–17	New Zealand	3	2
307	03–Mar–17	South Korea	0	2
308	06–Mar–17	Austria	3	1
309	08–Mar–17	Wales	0	0
310	11–Apr–17	Belgium	0	5
311	09–Jun–17	Romania	2	0
312	13–Jun–17	Sweden	0	1
313	07–Jul–17	Republic of Ireland	1	0
314	19–Jul–17	England	0	6
315	23–Jul–17	Portugal	1	2
316	27–Jul–17	Spain	1	0
317	14–Sep–17	Hungary	3	0
318	19–Oct–17	Belarus	2	1
319	24–Oct–17	Albania	5	0
320	19–Jan–18	Norway	0	3
321	22–Jan–18	Russia	0	0
322	03–Mar–18	New Zealand	2	0
323	06–Mar–18	New Zealand	2	0
324	05–Apr–18	Switzerland	0	1

Firhill Stadium, Glasgow
Ajdovščina Stadium, Ajdovščina
Fir Park, Motherwell
FFM Training Centre, Skopje
St Mirren Park, Paisley
Prioritet Serneke Arena, Gothenburg
Falkirk Stadium, Falkirk
St Mirren Park, Paisley
Falkirk Stadium, Falkirk

FC Minsk Stadium, Minsk
Laugardalsvöllur, Reykjavik
Almondvale Stadium, Livingston
GSZ Stadium, Larnaca
Tasos Marko Stadium, Paralimni
A Papadopoulos Stadium, Larnaca
GSP Stadium, Nicosia
Makario Stadium, Nicosia
Tasos Markou Stadium, Paralimni
Den Dreef, Leuven

Falkirk Stadium, Falkirk
Myresjöhus Arena, Växjö
Stark's Park, Kirkcaldy
Stadion Galgenwaard, Utrecht
Het Kasteel, Rotterdam
De Adelaarshorst, Deventer
Telki Training Centre, Telki
FC Minsk Stadium, Minsk
St Mirren Park, Paisley
La Manga Stadium, La Manga

Pinatar Arena, Murcia
La Manga Stadium, La Manga
La Manga Stadium, La Manga
LIPO Park, Schaffhausen

325	10–Apr–18	Poland	3	0
326	07–Jun–18	Belarus	2	1
327	12–Jun–18	Poland	3	2
328	30–Aug–18	Switzerland	2	1
329	04–Sep–18	Albania	2	1
330	13–Nov–18	USA	0	1
331	17–Jan–19	Norway	1	3
332	21–Jan–19	Iceland	1	2
333	01–Mar–19	Canada	0	1
334	04–Mar–19	Iceland	4	1
335	06–Mar–19	Denmark	1	0
336	05–Apr–19	Chile	1	1
337	08–Apr–19	Brazil	1	0
338	28–May–19	Jamaica	3	2
339	09–Jun–19	England	1	2
340	14–Jun–19	Japan	1	2
341	19–Jun–19	Argentina	3	3
342	30–Aug–19	Cyprus	8	0
343	08–Nov–19	Albania	5	0
344	04–Mar–20	Ukraine	3	0
345	07–Mar–20	Iceland	1	0
346	10–Mar–20	Northern Ireland	2	1
347	23–Oct–20	Albania	3	0
348	27–Oct–20	Finland	0	1
349	27–Nov–20	Portugal	0	1
350	01–Dec–20	Finland	0	1
351	19–Feb–21	Cyprus	10	0
352	23–Feb–21	Portugal	0	2
353	10–Jun–21	Northern Ireland	1	0
354	15–Jun–21	Wales	1	0
355	17–Sep–21	Hungary	2	0
356	21–Sep–21	Faroe Islands	7	1
357	22–Oct–21	Hungary	2	1

St Mirren Park, Paisley
Falkirk Stadium, Falkirk
Kielce City Stadium, Kielce
St Mirren Park, Paisley
Loro Boriçi Stadium, Shkodër
St Mirren Park, Paisley

La Manga Stadium, La Manga
La Manga Stadium, La Manga
Estádio Municipal, Lagos
Estádio Municipal da Bela Vista, Parchal
Estádio Algarve, Sao Joao da Venda
Pinatar Arena, Murcia
Pinatar Arena, Murcia
Hampden Park, Glasgow
Stade de Nice, Nice
Roazhon Park, Rennes

Parc des Princes, Paris
Easter Road, Edinburgh
Elbasan Arena, Elbasan
Pinatar Arena, Murcia
Pinatar Arena, Murcia
Pinatar Arena, Murcia
Tynecastle Park, Edinburgh
Bolt Arena, Helsinki
Estádio do Restelo, Lisbon
Easter Road, Edinburgh

AEK Arena, Larnaca
Papadopoulos Stadium, Larnaca
Seaview, Belfast
Parc y Scarlets, Llanelli
Hidegkuti Stadium, Budapest
Hampden Park, Glasgow
Hampden Park, Glasgow

358	26–Oct–21	Sweden	0	2
359	26–Nov–21	Ukraine	1	1
360	30–Nov–21	Spain	0	8
361	16–Feb–22	Wales	1	3
362	19–Feb–22	Slovakia	2	0
363	22–Feb–22	Hungary	0	0
364	12–Apr–22	Spain	0	2
365	24–Jun–22	Ukraine	4	0
366	02–Sep–22	Netherlands	1	2
367	06–Sep–22	Faroe Islands	6	0
368	06–Oct–22	Austria	1	0
369	11–Oct–22	Republic of Ireland	0	1
370	14–Nov–22	Venezuela	2	1
371	15–Feb–23	Iceland	0	2
372	18–Feb–23	Philippines	2	1
373	21–Feb–23	Wales	1	1
374	07–Apr–23	Australia	1	0
375	11–Apr–23	Costa Rica	4	0
376	14–Aug–23	Northern Ireland	3	0
377	18–Aug–23	Finland	2	1
378	22–Sep–23	England	1	2
379	26–Sep–23	Belgium	1	1
380	27–Oct–23	Netherlands	0	4
381	31–Oct–23	Netherlands	0	1
382	01–Dec–23	Belgium	1	1
383	05–Dec–23	England	0	6

St Mirren Park, Paisley
Hampden Park, Glasgow
Estádio de La Cartuja, Seville

Pinatar Arena, Murcia
Pinatar Arena, Murcia
La Manga Stadium, La Manga
Hampden Park, Glasgow
Stadion Miejski, Rzeszow
Mac3Park Stadium, Zwolle
Tórsvøllur, Tóorshavn
Hampden Park, Glasgow
Hampden Park, Glasgow
Estádio Antonio Barbadillo, Arcos

Pinatar Arena, Murcia
Pinatar Arena, Murcia
Pinatar Arena, Murcia
Cherry Red Records Stadium, London
Hampden Park, Glasgow
Dens Park, Dundee
Tampere Stadium, Tampere
Stadium of Light, Sunderland
Hampden Park, Glasgow
Goffertstadion, Nijmegen

Hampden Park, Glasgow
Den Dreef, Leuven
Hampden Park, Glasgow

Uncovering Hidden Histories
Karen Fraser
A companion piece to 'The Challenges Of Re(Writing)
Women's Football History'

GIVEN THE NATURE of this book I do not need to talk
about why football is important but I do want to take a moment
to underline why the study of the history of women's football is
important. In order to understand any aspect of history, the
experience, perspective and influence of the whole population is
required. Recounting the history of women playing football
gives women and girls the opportunity to learn their stories, the
adversities they overcame and the challenge that participation
in football makes to socially-constructed gender norms.

When I first told people that I was going to be researching the
history of women's football in Scotland since the 1960s, a very
common response was 'Well that won't take you long'. While it
was said with a smile, most of those saying it believed there was
little women's football in Scotland before the 2000s and so
therefore, not much for me to research.

To be fair, as I set off on my journey, if these people had read
any of the previous writing about women's football in the
40-year period between 1960 and 2000, it did paint a picture of
very limited participation. The common description was of a
handful of teams playing in the 1960s and that following the
formation of the Scottish Women's Football Association
(SWFA) in 1972, there was a very slow growth across the years.
There was mention of a small growth spurt up in the 1990s
until the development of the women's premier league in 2000
led to the emergence of Scottish women's football in the public
consciousness. In addition, the women I spoke to at the start of
my research, who had played in the 1960s and 1970s were
themselves not aware of more than a handful of teams.

For a while, I too held on to this picture, after all to paraphrase

Andy Mitchell's comment in his piece on Scottish Women's internationals, researching the history of Scottish women's football is a challenge! Spurred on by historians of the women's game I met, I began a process of scouring local and national newspapers, personal archives and the SWFA papers I was able to track down. This will be an on-going process but I am committed to uncovering details of as many teams as possible. As a companion to Andy's search for the international matches, I am searching for both league and non-league teams across the period.

However, for me the search is not limited to the names, numbers, league and stats. One place to start to uncover the experiences of the women who played and so build knowledge about the history of women's football in Scotland which has been under reported and therefore under celebrated. I am fascinated by the stories that the women have to tell. These do often involve barriers and challenges but all the women I have interviewed have a common love of playing the game which comes across in their stories and the beaming smiles that emerge as they recount their adventures.

The term 'oral history interview' is the name given to process of talking to people to gather information about either their lives or specific experiences within them in order to preserve the details. Within the area of sports history, researchers realised the importance of gathering information in this way as for many marginalised groups, written records are either incomplete or non-existent. This approach is particularly important when researching the history of women's sports as the written records are often scarce as it provides access to women's hidden and ignored lives. In addition, oral histories can give new and valuable perspectives on women and the challenges they faced and choices they made.

While my initial research project has ended, I have continued to undertake oral history interviews in order to capture details of the lived experience of women who played football from 1960 onwards. I have identified additional women to interview through my work on the project to award retrospective Scotland Caps and through events and publicity around my research. Collecting this information from the women is important because their resilience, determination and resistance to constraints, provided the foundations of today's growing women's and girls' football community. These interviews reveal a narrative that pushes back against the association of football in Scotland with men and recognises and celebrates the voices of women who have largely gone unheard.

The purpose of the interviews I undertake with women players is to explore their memories, experiences and inspirations. To ensure that the women I speak to have every opportunity to share their stories, I aim for a free flow guided 'conversation' with the interviewee doing the majority of the talking and my role being to ask initial open questions with follow up prompts eliciting explanation or expansion. The intention is that the women should be able to tell their story in as much depth as they want, in the style they prefer and to concentrate on the parts they feel to be important with minimal direction or guidance from me. I generally have some topics that I want to cover but other than those, what the women choose to speak about and focus on in recounting their experience is up to them. This approach enables me, and future researchers, to hear the voices of the women involved talking about their experiences with their own words, emphasis and emotion. I produced a guide that I used during the interviews to ensure that, while encouraging the free flow of information, I would be able to cover the points that I was particularly interested in. The broad topics that I wanted to cover related to how the narrator became involved in women's football; the story of their involvement; what it meant to them and whether they were still involved. To assist with the discussion, I prepared prompt questions to use, if required, to stimulate recollections.

With the woman's permission the interviews were recorded to enable comprehensive collection of information and the facilitation of free-flowing discussion without the need for many handwritten notes.

At the end of the interview, I ask two questions that relate to the wider social context at the time the narrator was involved in women's football. Having explored attitudes they encountered whilst playing, I ask them whether they felt they were making any kind of statement about women's roles and rights by playing football. I also asked if they had a view about the development of women's football in Scotland and how this may have differed from other countries. The purpose of these questions is to explore whether resisting dominant norms was a motivator; whether the wider state of women's football was of interest to them; whether they had, indeed, given the situation any consideration and whether their perspective could offer any particular insights. I endeavoured to word these questions in a way that was exploratory and did not have a right or wrong answer.

Frequently when I first communicate with the women, they will say that they are happy to be interviewed but do not think they have much to tell. However, once we start, invariably the women have a wealth of stories and experiences to recount, being proud of their achievements and pleased to contribute to the history with tales of their love of playing football. My hope is that by undertaking oral history interviews with individuals I can use their recollections to indicate areas in which I might seek new information. As a result, my engagement with archive and interview research means that each lead to potential areas of research in the other.

It is important to speak to women about when they played, what teams they played with and what influenced those choices. It is, however, equally important as Andy explained, to take account of the ways in which information is remembered, the meanings attached to it and how it compares with other sources.

I have encountered examples where the recollection of the women does not tie in with written sources of information. At times it has been appropriate and straightforward to ask about this but at other times I have left it and addressed the issue in my own written record.

Finally, I ask my interviewee if there was anything that they wanted to add or anything that they had thought I would ask about but had not. The purpose of this is to give further opportunity for them to talk about what was of importance to them and to be able to include it, even if I had not introduced it as a topic.

My perception is that the women have a pleasant experience during the interview, with them at ease and given the opportunity to expand on their points of interest. This has been confirmed both by immediate verbal feedback from the women, the smiles and laughter that happened during interviews. In addition, many have encouraged other women to take come forward to be interviewed.

The oral history testimonies that I am collecting, provide a significant contribution to knowledge about women's football in Scotland since the 1960s. They are being used to provide information for inclusion in articles, books and presentations.

This is really good for increasing knowledge about the extent of women's football in Scotland during this time but I also want to ensure that as wide as possible an audience can access the stories the interviews contain. To achieve this, I am working to build an archive of the recordings, transcriptions and summaries of the information. Where there is limited existing material but an opportunity to gather information about lived experiences, then it is possible to use oral history interviews to create an archive. The major advantage is that the oral histories offer up information that is not available elsewhere and afford the possibility of creating an archive rather than adapting an existing one.

What I want to achieve is the collection of accounts from women at every level of women's football since the 1960s, to counter their exclusion from the narrative and amplify their voices by telling their stories. The intention is that these will provide insight into women's resistance to the dominant subject of conversation within football and encourage the exploration of subjects that have not previously been valued within the Scottish football community.

This work is ongoing and the interviews provide a vivid description of the lived experiences of the women who played football in Scotland during the past 60 years, including the challenges and opportunities encountered by them. Most importantly they provide a voice to the women who for too long have not been heard and equally remind everyone that women's football has been a vibrant part of Scottish life for much longer than previously recorded.

BRAVEHEARTS

Graeme Brown

A tartan tale like no other,
written through the years,
Elsie, Edna and Rose,
one of them won the World Cup,
didn't you hear?

Oh Rose, you are a Scottish legend,
a World Cup, Serie A and Ballon d'Or
Those images are the greatest
but why are there no other Scots,
there to score?

Ah that's a long, long story
however the answer is very short
we were trapped in a man's world
but our freedom has been brought.

Many menfolk haven't managed
what Shelley Kerr has done
Vogts, Smith, McLeish, Burley, Levein and
Strachan
they tried often without success,
but we remember them,
nonetheless.

Sitting in Hampden's playground,
Scotland's Theatre of Dreams
The children chorus and roar,
creaks it at the seams
Kerr's Pinks Army stride out to hallowed field
Where Cuthbert's thunderbolt is daringly new,
A father's daughter cries with joy
screaming 'Daddy, that flew'
Another tartan army diehard,
is born Hampden new.

And now we are celebrating,
Scotland has made it through
A pontoon of years
since our last French trip was seen
on a mission to pass the group
and find a place,
Scotland has never been

O Land of Whiskied Thistle,
our bravest lassies are here,
our Girls, are playing our Game,
with the bravest hearts
amid a sea of saltire cheer.

Watching from Football's heaven
Scotch Professors gather once more
Captain Campbell reminds those English games,
Watson laughs amid gathering cheer
They didn't see us coming in those days,
victories were our only way,

we are coming to France to find you,
we are coming to support you once more.

Once, we were the Football Kings
teaching the world the combination,
regardless of age or gender,
football shall never again surrender,
the Queens of Football
are here,
forevermore.

Campbell turns to Henry Smith,
asking for a final prayer.
The first Football Poet stands once more:

Go on Scotland,
Helter Skelter,
on you Pelter,

Go on Scotland,
we pray for a Belter,
play out our hopes and dreams.

THIS TEAM IS FOR MY DAUGHTER

Laura Carberry

To show her she's allowed to be different
and to dae the things they said are no for her
because she's a her.

This team is for me.
As I remember being telt I hid to wear
a skirt to school and that the fitba team wis fir boys
so I played keepy-ups with a netball.

This team is for my Granny
who couldny watch her beloved team in the pub,
because why would she like fitba?
She wis a wummin!

This team is for all the wee lassies
who pull up their socks and punt the ba' on a cauld
dour,
damp Scottish day and play fae the heart.

This team is for the lassies who score
and dae the Hampden run,
imagining the songs that will be sung
about them by the Tartan Army,

before they head hame to get telt aff
fur the state eh them.
This team is fur all the wee lassies
who widny be telt that fitba wis just fur the boys

and their dreams coming true
tae the soundtrack of Flower of Scotland.

HOLD THE FRONT PAGE

Gayle Smith

As a new campaign begins
seeds of hope are planted
emerging names are given

their colours
and a chance to liven up
the squad

Fresh faces of youth mingle
with the older more
experienced players.
Prayers are offered
for Jenna and Lauren
that new stars will be born in
Scotland jerseys
and a better harvest will be grown
this time than last.

Those were barren nights
when we wilted on frosty
evenings
more suited for cups of coffee
and comfort TV
than grinding out results
in games
which would have been played earlier
had we not been plagued
by events we could never
have foreseen

Now a changed team
starts afresh
as some less familiar names
take the stage
the manager tells the press to
hold the front page
there are headlines waiting to
be written
and you are the girls to
write them.

BELIEVERS

Kevin Graham

Qualification was once a given
There was never a thought of us missing out

Our place was the comfort of the underdog
on the undercard
Where we never said die,
We worked so hard,
We brought colour and spirit over finesses
It's what we did best

All the rampant lions and lionesses
Wearing dark blue
All feeling blessed
That we were coming down the road

You would hear the noise
of us coming down the road
you would feel our pride
of our wee land
a nation that never demands
but dreams more than any other.

A nation of dreamers, schemers
And forever believers

So let's believe again.

SCOTLAND, OUR SCOTLAND

Julie McNeill

It's fair to say we're all feeling the trudge
no sun-soaked, saltire-draped adventures
in the offing.

That Erin Cuthbert strike at the Parc de Princes
feels like another time, another life,
Our pre-Corona.

Go on!
Heat up the pie
get the colours on,

slosh hot liquid in the homemade Bovril
and treat yourself to 90 minutes of hope.
Goodness knows, we need it.

Here we go! Can you picture it though?
Silverware glinting in the early evening sun
Shelley Kerr thanking everyone,

Elmslie, Weir and Arnot, arms aloft
crowds crowing and congratulating
in pre-pandemic full-on hugs

and Scotland, our Scotland, arms locked
raising all of us up.

Bairns & Lassies

This section celebrates the future of the game, our bairns and lassies. We reflect on the excitement that the game represents to young girls past and present. From recalling the thrill of going to their first match to their passion for playing the beautiful game.

GIRL FOOTBALLER

Jackie Kay

The ball soars and the ball flies.
The ball goes up. The ball goes in.
And the balls in your eyes are
rolling and spinning,
spinning and rolling.
And the blood in your heart is singing.

You feel yourself whirl and twirl.
What a talented girl.
Nothing like this feeling you get
when the ball bulges in the back of the net.
No, you don't easily forget
the sweet sweet taste of a goal.
Replay it in your mind again:

Left foot in the air, flick,
straight to the back of the net.
Play it again and again
- the ball's beautiful roll to the goal.
Nothing like the soaring and roaring
when the plump ball hits the thin net.
And the sad blue goalie sits on the sad green grass.
The look on the slow face,

watching the ball go past, fast.
No chance. No chance. Watching the ball dance.
You dribble from the midfield down.
You get past three men.
You do a chip, a volley, you curl the ball.
You perm the air with your talent, and all
the fans sizzle and spark,
all the fans sing and dance,
football is one long romance
with the ball, with the ball and all.

You nutmeg the goalie like the goalie is a spice.
You get the ball in, not once, twice, but thrice!
Hat trick! You make the goalie feel sick.
So you lie down and roll in celebration.
You feel the team jump on your back
then you feel the whole nation,
goggle-eyed in admiration.
You squeeze your fist,
like this, like a kiss, to the wild crowd
and your football of a heart is bouncing and proud.

WHEELER

Elsie Cook

You can keep Peter Shilton, Pat Jennings, and the rest
cos we know oor goalie's easy the best
she joined Stewarton Thistle when jist a young lass
wi her pal Lynda Broon – whom none could surpass

Fae mony a tussle we'd emerge wae ease –
thanks mainly tae Pamela's expertise
crossballs, free kicks, she deals wae them all
Her only real difficulty's in buildin' her wall..

'Move over left..no!...a little more right...
that's it Jeannie, keep the wa tight!'
But the wa chickened oot tae Spartan's delight,
a gap emerged which gave Pam a fright

The centre's hard shot fair flew through the space
but Pamela was there wae a save that wis ace.
Wan day at Hurlford's Blair Park, whilst trainin,
the forwards on Pamela their shots were rainin...

'Hit them hard!' says Elsie, 'Aim for the crossbar!'
Mair practice wae high balls and she'd really go far...
But someone let fly wae a real humdinger
which Pamela tipped ower – but broke her wee finger!

She takes mony a knock, and mony a bump
and lands oan her rearend, wae mony a thump...
It's a famous rearend which is second tae none
for she's also reknowned fir showin her bum!

She's a real big joker aff the park tae
withoot big Wheeler, whit wid we dae?
We aw hold Pamela in the highest esteem
withoot ye hen, we'd only have hauf a team.

That's why Pamela, we'd aw like tae say..
'Awrabest hen on yer 17th Birthday!'

CAILEAGAN NAN COUNTY 2023

Lynsey Gilmour

Lasan ann an gruaidhean,
Sùilean cuilmeanach le aiobhneas,
Arm nan nigheanan,
Cho salach ri mùcan
Cho sona ri brogan

Thig iad gach seachdainn,
'S ann o fheadh à tha iad,
Rosach, Catach, Gallach, Sgitheanach,
Siubhail iad a' Ghàidhealtachd
Air a fad, is air a leud.

Còmhla cruinn
Uile san aon staing,
Tog inntinn, tog chridhe
Leotha an latha,
Thig beò air an geama

Uair no uair-eigin
Thig tioma air iad
Far an àite
An do chuir iad seachad
Laithean geala

Ach an drastaich
Chan eil dad ach,
Càirdeas, còmhstrì
Drùidhte anns an t-uisge
No greadadh na grèine

Sùilean cuilmeanach le aiobhneas,
Lasan ann an gruaidhean
Salach agus sona.

THE GIRLS OF COUNTY 2023

Lynsey Gilmour

Cheeks flushed,
Eyes bright
An army of girls,
Filthy as pigs,
Happy as shoes.

They arrive each week
They come from all over
Ross, Sutherland, Caithness, Skye,
Travelling the length and breadth
Of the Highlands.

They come,
In the struggle together.
Lift spirits, lift hearts,
The day theirs,
They live for the game.

In time
They'll grow nostalgic,
For the place
 they spent
Their glory days.

But now,
Friendship, rivalry
Soaked by rain
Burnt by sun

There is nothing
But eyes shining with joy
Filthy and cheerful.

LUTON

Elsie Cook

Stewarton Ladies ventured south
to represent Scotland, their hearts in their mouths
to take on all comers, in the British Fives
a weekend tae remember, the rest o' their lives

At last we arrived in London's bright lights
an decided we'd spend time, seeing the sights
like all good tourists we visited 'Tooshie's'
an saw aw the ghouls wae blood oan their moothies

Tae oor hotel and we eight, booked in swift
while oor fans and oor punk, slipped intae the lift,
we cheated the staff aw the time we were there...
Shame oor supporters had tae sleep oan the flair

Sheona got lumbers three or four
but some o' the others couldnae keep score!
Allison and Ruby had tae think again
when Elsie said, and meant it, 'Lights oot at ten!'

Morning came and breakfast too
when a plan was laid by this motley crew..
'We all sat watching as Elsie grew bolder
...and slowly opened her light blue folder'

Toast and eggs and sausages too
disappeared intae that folder blue..
Our loyal supporters enjoyed this class fare
Wae wee Shirley askin', 'Mum, any mair?'

We teamed up wae the Irish boys, shared their big bus
arrived at the venue withoot any fuss
feenished the day, tap o' oor section
then pointed oorselves in the leisure direction

On the disco flair, the lights were flashin
an Christine thocht her handsome wee partner, was
smashing'!
The finals arrived and having had a guid rest
We were ready, we thocht, tae take oan Britain's best

Wae the cheers o' the English ringing in the air
Oor disco connections were definitely there..
'C'MOAN ya wee cracker...' wis the Irish drole
Wae oor Pakistani disco pals, shouting, 'Geev us a goal!'

At one point wee Broon thought it the end of her
career...
Wee soul suffered aw day, fae DIAHORREAH!
But alas having given of oor very best...
We were forced tae third place, knocked oot by the
winners,
England's northwest

But oor adventure in London was not yet done
we left oor punk on Platform One.
She then challenged Catherine tae an escalator race
which resulted on Lorna, oor punk, fallin' flat on her
face

Jeannie laughed so much, that meenits later
she drapped her case on the elevator
and there, in Charing Cross underground station
lay aw Jeannie's undies on view tae the nation

Big Wheeler, in fits, got in on the act
laughed so much, missed her footing, she took a step
back.
Then tae Pamela's utter dismay
the moving stairs cairrit her away

Back hame in Scotland, it all seemed a dream
as we think of the Champions we might have been!

BECKY BOOTS

Elsie Cook

The first time I spied wee Becky was on the back o' Gibby's bike...
a three year old, cheeky, tousle-haired tyke
and I knew she was special the minute I saw
like Gibby, wee Becky could haundle a baw

She had so much skill, I had tae see more, so I found masel
Chappin at Lucy, her mammy's, front door!
At seven she signed oan for Stewarton,
the wee-est defender ye ever did see

There wis nothin at aw this wee star did lack
an' wae Stewarton Thistle young team, she never looked back.
She could control, lay aff with inimitable style
but it wis her coolness in defence that made us aw smile.

Wae her blonde hair in wee bunches and an impish grin
a wee slip o' a lass wae legs faur too thin!
But opponents, much bigger, soon found, they couldnae get past
her immaculate timing's never been surpassed.

Wae the wee 'Julie's', Smith and Watson, Linda Lindsay,
young Lulubelle
this wee under nines team did really well
in every tourney, they swept the boards
and Becky's wee Stewarton team's reputation, soared!

Dae yooz remember yon 5's at Perth's Bell Centre
we arrived 5 minutes late and 'jobsworth' widnae let us enter
'Becky, and Sharron, you're the wee-est, come wae me, an stert
greetin -
let them see yer upset and they might let us in!'

But, did they? Did they heck, 'cos they knew we wid win!

223

JEANNIE' 1978

Elsie Cook

For Jean Harkins one of the very best Scottish
central midfielders I've ever seen.

At the tender age of nine or ten – a wee lassie asked tae
get a gemme

'I think hen,' says me, 'yer a wee bit wee, but gie's a baw and
let me see.'

Wee Jeannie proved up tae the test, in the shade she left
the rest
there wis naethin' wae a baw she couldnae dae –

so intae the wee team she wis pit tae play!
There wae her pals – the Corbett twins

they led Stewarton ontae successive wins.
Wae Izzy (Blades) an' 'Budgie' (wee Lynn Watson), an' wee
Alli Black

There wis nothing this young team did lack.
The opposition wis left in mony a fankle

when the twins and wee Jeannie played their 'triangle'
The teams' reputation soon spread far and wide

and every boys club wanted tae tak oan this great side.
An invite fae Hamburg in Germany

sent Stewarton packin' and aff tae sea.
Once oan board boat, wae the boys of the 'Annick'

Elsie and 'Pinky' began tae panic.
The boys were in wan cabin – the lassies next door

'God, Pinky!' Says Elsie, pacin' the floor.
We'll need tae keep a watchful eye –

cos the boys on cider were gettin' high!
'Lock yer doors girls, bed by ten...

if yooz don't, I'll let Boab Nisbet ken'
The lights went out and all went quiet...

'Phew!' Says 'Pinky', 'I'd feared a riot'
Then a wee giggle broke the night air.

'It's comin' fae cabin sixteen!' I gasp, in despair!
The door burst open – and there, swingin' her legs,

sat wee Jeannie, oan wan o' the boys tap bunk beds.

'We wis jist talkin' tactics' she was heard tae claim.

'Honest a wis...don't send me hame!'
Noo once in Hamburg they were aw separated
an' Jeannie wis sent hame wae a fat man she hated,
but once these problems were aw cleared up

The lassies played great fitba and lifted the cup!

GOALIE GLOVES

Jane Patience

Standing, cold between the posts.
Eleven years of tiny muscle, unfused bone.
Daring them to do their worst
You brace yourself to take their kicks
You stand alone.
Skinny arms made Minnie Mouse
by giant goalie gloves,
your ticket to respect.
Although you start to notice now
and so do they,
the budding breast and narrowing waist.
The slender length of neck and gentle clavicle
slope.
So you scarf up and pad out,
but cannot hide the pout,
the upturned Cupid's bow,
the subtle grace of every throw.
An azure flash from underneath each lengthy lash.
Resilient, hard and tough,
You're one of them for now,
But Sweet, I'll tell you this -
Your boyish days are numbered
and it won't be long
before you know what strength is.
The girls team beckons to you.
I know for now that makes you scoff
but womanhood approaches fast.
That's when the gloves come off.

IN THEIR OWN WORDS
Collected by Karen Fraser

ANOTHER FACET of women's football, up until the early 1990s, was the absence of youth teams which resulted in young girls seeking out senior teams to play for. This was often beneficial for the team, as the younger players were enthusiastic and regular attendees, and assisted in reaching enough players on the team. However, the wide age range meant that the team members had to take responsibility for the safety of the younger players, which could be challenging at times, especially on trips to away matches.

Here are some comments from women about their experience:

> [It was a] young team, no one could drive, went everywhere on a bus. So, my recollection is walking 45 mins to training, 45 mins back as I didn't have the money for bus fares, I walked everywhere, the training ground was also the meeting point for catching the bus on a Sunday. (Kate)
>
> My first official game for East Fife, aged eleven, was against Edinburgh Dynamos who were the team at the time. Sheila Begbie was marking me and the first thing I done was to nutmeg her and score a goal. She came up and shook my hand, which was really good. (Susan)
>
> The expectation from my mother was that they would look after me given that we were going to play in a national league. I remember the first time we were going to cross the bridge and play in Edinburgh; she was not for letting me travel or go without signed consent, cos she felt it was too far for daughter to go with a group of adults. (Pauline).

> I've played football since I can remember. I love everything about the game, talking about it, watching it, thinking about it and of course playing it. I joined the Dundee Strikers when I was fourteen years of age and I thought it was great to play for a girls' team after playing the game so long at school, with all the boys. When I found out there was a team for women, I was in heaven. (Linda)

Kate Cooper who has been involved from the 1980s to date. She played at elite club level and was a volunteer committee member for SWF. She is currently a club coach for an SWFL club.

Linda Gellatly who was involved in the 1970s and 1980s. She played at elite club level and for the SWNT.

Pauline McDonald who has been involved from 1980s to date. She played at elite club level in Scotland, England and the USA. She also captained the SWNT and qualified as a coach. She is the former head coach of the Scottish Under-17s National Squad and is due to take up the role of inaugural head coach for Dallas Trinity FC who are set to join the new USL Super League that starts in August 2024.

Susan Williams who was involved from the mid-1970s through to early 1990s. She played at semi-serious club level.

FOOTERING ABOOT

Jane George

Lassies playin' fitba, whatever next Jimmy!
They'll be wantin' the vote and jobs wi 'pensions!
Naw naw we mebbe tolerated it durin' the war
aye everybody had to dae their bit then,
even ma maw worked in munitions.

Gracie and Maggie wis tellin' me
they startit a fitba team
wi' the ither lassies
Cannae quite believe it masel'
so thocht I wid just hae a keek through the gates
an' it's true!

There they were kickin' a ba' aboot
an making no' a bad job o' it.
Ah've heard tell they startit a league an' even play wi'
ither lassies an get a bit o' a crowd!
Hey Jimmy dae ye fancy goin' for a look?

Might be better than the 'Gers the wey they're
playin' right noo
Jist dinnae tell the wife Alec or she micht want tae
join as weel!

KNITTING IT TOGETHER
Corrie Campbell

I STARTED my football journey like many other women, playing with the boys at school with very limited opportunities for females to enjoy the sport I jumped at the chance to play in the schoolyard.

The first taste I got of some of the inequalities and barriers in football for women and girls was the janitor at my primary school saying I wasn't allowed to play for the school team despite the boys wanting me to. Why? Because I was a girl!

Girls did...wait for it...*knitting* (!) while the boys played football. Luckily, I had supportive parents who championed my love for the game and pulled me out of knitting class. I didn't get to go out on the pitch though – this energetic sport-loving girl was sent to the library to read books instead.

When I moved to high school the opportunities open to girls were still few and far between. That is until David Proven, the local football development officer, carved out a mixed community football session on a Friday afternoon. I lived for this wee window of time where I could run and play the game I loved.

When I was sixteen, I undertook my coaching qualifications which, ironically, was the time I actually learned how to play the game in a team. I had never played eleven-a-sides or been part of my own team so this learning curve was steep but transformative.

It wasn't until I learned to drive that I could access a women's team. I travelled to Johnstone to play for the women's team and they were – women! I still felt like a very young girl and remember being quite intimidated by playing with adults but so excited to finally be amongst other females who loved to play like I did.

There were still huge barriers – lack of facilities, miles

between games and sometimes it felt like an uphill struggle but we were playing! It was wonderful.

At nineteen, I moved to London and had the life-changing opportunity to play for West Ham Women's Team. Better facilities, better opportunities and it felt like a real watershed moment.

My experience has driven me to work in education, through Active Schools and then for the Scottish Football Association. I want no young girl to be sent to the library instead of the football pitch (despite the brilliant and transformative resource libraries can be). I am determined to champion sport for women and girls and to build structures and supports that keep enjoyment and opportunity at the centre of football for all women and girls.

In my lifetime, I have watched the SWNT qualify for the World Cup and some great advances in women's grassroots football. I'm hopeful for the future, but we've still got a distance to travel – I'm due to play 5's on Sunday and the venue confirmed they only have shower facilities for men!

We will keep fighting the fight, inch by inch because change is made in such ways.

Thank you to all the women and girls who have laid the ground before me, I hope that the legacy of my generation is that the battles can be fought out on the pitch, not on the road to get there.

NAE JUIST GREGORY'S GIRL

David Kilpatrick

Speil th' tape ower 'n' ower again
Whit urr ye peepin', lassie
Ye fancy that laddie
Yi'll waant tae be his, dae ye
Haunless dunderheided Gregory
Ye fancy a laddie lik' that

Och th' twa o' ye wid mak' a braw match
Yi'll waant tae speil bawwi' him
Thay roar 'n' roar

Ye speil th' tape ower 'n' ower again
Bit thay dinnae ken how come ye'r peepin'
Ye dream o' days oan rid blaes

Nae hugs 'n' kisses or romance, na
Nae wee jimmies
Ta speil fitba

Is a' ye care aboot
Tae be Queen o' th' rid blaes
Nae juist Gregory's Girl

THE ONE WORD PASS:
FOR THE WOMEN'S TEAM

Janet Crawford

Faces lit up when asked for the quick one-word answer
like a perfectly drilled pass had crossed
consciousness
'What does football mean to you?'
the simple question asked
from the girls who'd trained for a month
to those with a quarter century of ball kicking joys...

all agreed this game, football – summed up life

the students said they let the rain during training
wash away their essay due date fears

the mums pulled up, rather than folded socks
then ran for a pass
no way were they letting life run past

the stuffiness of the 9-5, all agreed
was banished by the bounce of a ball
and the shout of *'push on, it's one all'*
on a green dream making pitch
whether match day light or evening training pod bright

where the lines help you to drive forward
rather than hold you in,
contained to the roles put upon you by life
even as the drizzle danced between their feet
smiles said it all
rain covers sat to the side
hiding nothing

LOVE AT FIRST SIGHT: THE DAY WOMEN'S FOOTBALL STOLE MY HEART
Margot McCuaig

I'LL NEVER FORGET the flood of noise, or the dryness in the back of my throat as football boots kicked up banks of dust. The intensity swept through me, stinging my skin, like I was paddling barefoot in a freezing sea. I was at the edge of the white line, within touching distance of an ocean of players, my sandshoes pinking with blaes, empty crisp packets circling my ankles. My two sisters and their teammates were on the pitch, scattered like bright shells on a beach. I had never seen anything like it before. It was a women's football match and everything about it was thrilling.

I was clasping my mum's hand, my fingers pressing into the softness of her palm. She was remonstrating with every kick of the ball, her arm flailing in and out, up and down, hauling me with her, my fingers stretching high towards a blanket of bright blue sky and then sinking hard against her thigh. I rocked on tiptoes to stay with her, my lips tight in case I cried out and extinguished anything of the moment. We had lit candles after all, in the chapel before the game, the Priest's new football team not yet blessed enough to rely on skill alone.

The match was intense but in brief spells of calm I gingerly placed my head on Mum's torso, taking in the men watching nearby, using their hands like skip caps to protect their narrow eyes from the glare of the sun. One gesticulated at our team, his head bobbing, angry words I could not hear hurtling from his mouth. My arm was yanked high in response, my toes barely touching ash as Mum spent loose words that sunk him into silence.

We scored a goal and I stretched my neck in triumph, tossing my ponytail to the side, my hand now free as Mum suspended our link to holler her support; short and sharp like a door slamming shut. There wasn't time to dwell. Conjoined again I used my free hand to finesse the hair that was stretched taut against my temples, wishing I was wearing a white headband, pulled down over my ears like my elder sister.

I think the match was in 1974, or maybe 1975. I was six or seven. Too young to play for the team. One of my sisters was around eleven or twelve, the other fourteen or fifteen. I won't ask them to confirm, as this is my memory. The day I fell in love with women's football.

Our team was called St Gabriel's. Formed, I think, in response to the lifting of the 'ban'. The game took place nearby, at Our Lady of the Missions.

I'd been to football many times. I was a regular visitor to Celtic Park with my siblings and parents. I knew football. I loved football. But as a girl it was a game I played with my twin brother in the garden, or in the school playground on the brief occasions I was fortunate enough to be picked by the boys for an unorganised lunchtime battle. Never on a pitch, never as part of an eleven-a-side team, and never just with girls. That had been unthinkable. But now, as I watched my sisters, I could imagine playing in a team. A girls' team. Life was about to change and the feeling was exhilarating.

But it didn't change. At some point in the game the atmosphere became explosive. There was an accusation of male ringers in the opposition, and some players argued with their competitors. Spectator angst spilled over in icy waves. As the players left the pitch, an eerie silence engulfed us. It heralded both the start and the end of something.

'*Shameful*', said the Priest, '*this game is not for girls*'. An opinion obliterated the dream. Although I'm sure a band of men, skip cap hands shaking profusely, helped to seal our fate. I remember glancing at the Schoenstatt nuns who had been cheering our team, their dusty shoes hidden beneath the stark black and white of their habits. Perhaps it was a message from

God. There would be no grey area. It was over. I imagined them gathering long handled brooms, dusting red ash from the doorstep of the convent, their heads dizzy with the dissolution of freedom.

For a while I focused on my twin brother's matches, cheering him from behind the goal, the memory of that day sifting into the distance. But it wasn't disappearing. Love doesn't dissolve meekly. Gradually it shook violently inside me, unsettled and loosened, as un-still as the tides. Discontent rushed through me in waves, starting at the school hockey pitch where I angrily clutched my stick, observing my brothers as they freely played the game I wasn't allowed to participate in.

Finally, a realisation rose within. There must have been others. Women and girls who refused to be ruffled by disapproving glances and pronouncements of inappropriateness. They swelled my insides, demanding space, insisting I listen to their stories. When I studied for my undergraduate history degree, I searched for the girls I'd left behind. I pounded the results into the ether. I found stark inequalities and powerful narratives. And rousing pioneers who fought against the unscrupulous obstacles constantly put in the way of women's football. These transgressors did not accept *no*.

As I moved forward, my love deepened and so did my voice, becoming gravelly and strong with a determination to level the playing field. The wee girl who watched in awe as her sisters blazed a trail hadn't forgotten. Love didn't slip like sand through my fingers. It shapeshifted, spreading its intensity through me; a fine shingle, once upon a time made of dense stone.

TO THEM ALL

Jim Mackintosh

Tomorrow is a test born
a long time ago, only now
finding its feet on fresh grass.

I will hear doubt, derision and
celebrate none of their indignation
but move the horizon a little further.

I will embrace tomorrow, inventing
my own destiny, the one I share with
my sisters, the ones I love and with you.

At any time, in victory or defeat
it won't be strange to shed tears.
Images of rage, of division have no place.

> It is for us, now that the grass is confident
> to support our feet, to test tomorrow
> born a long time ago.

GRIEF

Gabrielle Barnby

Talking on about the game,
the details and the mistakes of officials dissected,
the end of the season, an excuse, the real reason
grief.

It gave everyone something to listen to as the
youngsters played their sport:
haphazard, skilled, defiant, angry.

'That's three bad decisions,
crucial decisions
that were wrong.'

Watch the ball,
in silence that's what we do,
when life is slow and sad and stopped.

There might not be a whistle,
the game simply end,
with a kick gone awry,
a crowd turning from the pitch.

A solemn and bemused procession home,
the six yard box,
the eighteen yard box,
empty.

Children hoisted down from shoulders,
where they once sailed,
left to walk
through a field of cloth legs
that break open to let them through;
heart in mouth
at the loss.

NOTE:
Orkney, September 2019 – This poem was written after the sad, sudden loss of one of the parents who regularly stood at my side, as we watched our children at football training.

IN MITHER'S FIT STEPS

Rose Macgregor

Sae ye want tae be a fitbaw player
Said the mither tae her lass.
A knock-kneed bandy dribbler
Kickin a baw aboot the grass.
Weel ah hope yer fine an fit
Takin PE at the schule.
Yeel need a lot o exercise
Or yeel luik a proper fool.

Huv ye thocht aboot this carefully
Is this whit ye want tae dae.
Cause it's gaun tae cost me plenty
Tae buy a strip fir hame an away.
Ah'm no the richest o mithers
But ah'll dae ma best fir you.
Tae help ye be a fitbaw player
An mak yer dreams cam true.

Ah'll stairt an save some money
An whyle yer at the schule
Ah'll try ma luck at spot the baw
Put a line oan wi the pools.
Ah'll even turn oan Radio Clyde
An enter yon cash register.
Tae 61 0 25 ah'll text an text
Being the biggest ever competitor.

An when ye've jined a fitbaw team
Scoring goals intae the net.
When playing loads o fixtures
starring oan the TV set.
Remember me, yer mither
An dinnae dare foirgett
the buit's that got ye stairted
nearly kicked me intae debt.

A GIRL'S FOOTBALL DREAM

Aylei Pickup

When I was six, I used to kick a ball
I started training and stood very tall
It was the girls' team I joined
But wasn't enough for me to enjoy

On a cold winter's day September 2017
I went for a trial for the boys team and wanted to scream
I did it I did it, I am so very proud
my heart was thumping and I shouted out loud

Nearly 4 years on and still in the same team
I have met many good friends and they all treat me like a queen
After all I am the girl of the squad
But when it comes to training they don't hold back they all trudge

Monday, Wednesday hard training nights
And also Sundays early morning match day vibes
I get up excited and cannot wait for what the game brings on
after a long week wait
To be in the team talk with my mates and even more excited to
be handed the captain armband it's just great

To look round to see my mum's big smile and I turned round
and kick off for a while
I run and run and pass the ball I run some more and WOW I
scored a goal

I eat, sleep and breathe football and it makes me the happiest
and proudest girl
My love will continue to grow with my team and bring on
11-a-sides
Harder training, more commitment and more of taking risks
in my stride

Hard work with the boys instead of playing with toys
Will land me a place in the ladies' race
For now follow my heart and dreams
I am still smiling, loving and fighting to my teens

I gave up my friends in the girls to be brave and strong
To better myself and will be back before long
I can only play till I am 16 then back to the girls
To continue my teens

My fight through this journey is all worthwhile
So many friends and done with such style
To hopefully land a place in Spartans ladies team
Then move on to the massive DREAM

ABOUT THE CONTRIBUTORS

Morag Anderson's second chapbook, *And I Will Make of You a Vowel Sound* (2024), won the Aryamati Poetry Prize. In 2023, she was the Federation of Writers Makar and poet-in-residence for the Birnam Book Festival. She is currently working with The Canmore Trust (a suicide prevention charity).

Gabrielle Barnby lives in Orkney and writes short stories, poetry and fiction. She facilitates creative discovery and writing groups with participants from eight to 80 and has a strong interest in writing for wellbeing.

Paul Beeson is an award-winning Edinburgh born actor and writer. He was a member of the BBC Writersroom's Voices 2020 – Scottish Voices.

Graeme Brown is the founder of The Hampden Collection. In 2017, he discovered the only map in existence of the 'World's First Purpose Built International Football Ground', the first Hampden Park. His mission is to preserve, protect and promote the wonderful story of all three Hampden Parks.

Isla Buchanan is 23 years old and soon to be a qualified mental health nurse. She is also a football referee and says that football saved her life. Football was there for her in some dark days and still keeps her going to this day.

With a 12-year tenure at the Scottish FA, **Corrie Campbell** has undertaken various influential roles. Initially, she championed the development of girls' and women's football, fostering inclusivity within the sport. Transitioning into the role of Club Development Manager, she supported community football clubs in their journey toward becoming social enterprises, emphasising their role in the community. In her most recent role as Football Social Responsibility Manager, her focus has shifted toward promoting social and environmental sustainability within Scottish football. Her professional journey underscores a dedicated commitment to football's holistic development, encompassing gender equality, community engagement and environmental responsibility.

Laura Carberry is a feminist, a football fan and an avid reader. She enjoys writing fiction with the occasional foray into poetry. She's Glasgow born and bred and currently works with children and young people with additional support needs whilst also completing a Masters in CBT.

Thomas Clark is a poet and writer who works mainly in the Scots language. He was poet-in-residence at Lowland League side Selkirk FC from 2015 to 2018.

Peter Clive lives in Glasgow and is a scientist working in the renewable energy sector. He has been published in *Causeway/ Cabhsair*, *The Poet's Republic*, *Dreich*, and elsewhere. Five collections of his poetry are available, *the end of the age of fire*, *stowaway*, *19 women*, *Crossing the Minch* and *Moonsong*.

Cat Cochrane is a writer and poet living in Glasgow's East End. Her first collection of short stories and poems, *Sugar Town*, was published in 2023, with a second poetry collection, *Sweet Tease*, launching in summer 2024. You'll find her performing her poems across Glasgow and beyond at open mic nights and poetry slams.

A fan of football her whole life, **Elsie Cook's** love of women's football started when she helped her mum form a team to play in a charity match. The team won, and she was hooked. Under her leadership, Stewarton Thistle became one of the top Scottish teams in the 1960s and early 1970s. She was a founder member of the Scottish Women's Football Association and organised the first international match held in Scotland in November 1972. She continues to be a fierce ambassador for the women's game.

Janet Crawford is a Falkirk based writer. She is a trustee of The Federation of Writers (Scotland). She has programmed for the Falkirk Storytelling Festival. Her poetry has been included in anthologies including *Nutmeg, SWNT Poets Society, Razur Cuts: Finest Cuts, Short & Sweet.* She's a very happy Stenhousemuir FC supporter!

Karen Fraser is an independent researcher associated with the University of Stirling. Her PhD research focused on the history of women's football in Scotland from 1960 to 2021. While she has worked on different aspects of the history of Scottish football, her focus remains seeking to uncover the untold history of women's football in Scotland. She has published articles, presented at conferences, and has contributed to television documentaries, radio programmes, museum exhibitions and newspaper articles.

Allan Gaw was a medical pathologist and is now an international award-winning writer. His short stories, non-fiction and poetry have been published widely. His debut poetry collection entitled *Love & Other Diseases* was published in 2023. He is also the author of the Dr Jack Cuthbert mystery series of novels.

For the last 30 years, **Jane George** taught courses in Scottish women's history for adult education programmes in Edinburgh. She also worked as a researcher in sports studies at Stirling University. Recently retired, she has now more time to listen to music, go to art exhibitions and write poetry.

Stuart Gibbs is a PhD student at Manchester Metropolitan University with his study project focusing on women's football. He is a contributor to football blogs and a regular speaker at sports history conferences.

Lynsey Gilmour is a poet, storyteller and spoken word performer from Easter Ross. Working in Scots, Gaelic and English, she is interested in exploring the landscape and languages of the Highlands, and the less often told stories of the people, particularly women, who live there.

Kevin Graham writes poetry for people who don't like poetry. He has two collections out: *Seven Years of Henrik* and *Smile: Celebrating Steve Clarke and Scotland*. He's been booed at gala days and has played Belladrum. He's been told his poetry offends other poets. He's not too fussed about that.

Maya Halcrow is thirteen and lives in Edinburgh. She started out playing for a boys team when she was five and now plays for Hibs U16s Next Gen. Maya's favourite football moment was going to Nice to watch Scotland play their first ever World Cup game. She wrote this poem when she was ten years old.

Lindsay Hamilton – not the former Rangers and St Johnstone goalie – but the 5 foot 2 founder of The Glasgow Football Tour.

Alistair Heather is a writer and presenter, and Dundee United season ticket holder. He writes for newspapers and magazines on culture, politics and travel, and presents documentaries on BBC Radio 4 and BBC Scotland television.

Linda Jackson is the founding editor of Seahorse Publications. Her own work includes *The Siren Awakes* (2020) and *The Cabinet* (2021). She is one of the poets in both *Wanderlust Women: 3 Poets* (2021/2022) and *Wanderlust Women: Extra Baggage* (2023), her second poetry collection, *Siren Calling*, will be out this summer. She is published in various anthologies, including *New Writing Scotland*, has been a creative writing tutor for 35 years and a lifelong musician.

Jackie Kay is a much loved and widely published Scottish poet and playwright. She was the Makar (National Poet) of Scotland from 2016–2021. Her latest collection *May Day* has just been released.

Stuart Kenny is an Edinburgh-based poet. He has enjoyed two sell-out Fringe runs at the Scottish Storytelling Centre, with 2018 cult hit 'The Space Gecko Project' and 2023's 'Bear With Me: A Polar Bear in Scotland'. His travel writing is published regularly by *The Guardian* and the BBC.

David Kilpatrick is Professor of English and Sport Management and Program Director of Sport Management at Mercy University in New York. He is the author of *Obrigado: A Futebol Epic* (2015) and *95 Theses on the Reformation of Football* (2022).

Steven Lawther is a Raith Rovers fan based in Edinburgh. His book *Arrival – How Scotland's Women Took Their Place on the World Stage and Inspired a Generation* was published by in 2021.

Hamish MacDonald's poetry has been included in many anthologies as well as in his own collection, *Wilson's Ornithology & Burds in Scot's* (2020). He is also known as a performance poet and is the Bankies Bard, the official poet of Clydebank Football Club.

Rose Macgregor is a retired nursery nurse who spends her time writing in Scots and English, in between caring for her disabled husband. She has been writing poetry since primary school and is a member of the Scots Language Society with poems published in their *Lallans* journals.

Jim Mackintosh is the author of seven poetry collections and editor/co-editor of four anthologies including *Mind the Time* (2017) in support of the Football Memories dementia groups. He was the first poet in the UK appointed to a professional football club – St Johnstone FC. From its launch in 2017 until 2022, he was the poetry editor of *Nutmeg* football magazine and between 2019 and 2022, Poet-in-Chief of The Hampden Collection. His latest collection, *We are Migrant*, was published in May 2024.

Keeks Mc is a Glaswegian performance and written poet, capturing her thoughts exclusively in her native tongue – colourful and descriptive Scots. Her work tackles contemporary topics, addressing pressing social and cultural issues and observations on daily life with a fresh and unique blend of humour, frankness and raw emotion.

Margot McCuaig, author of *The Birds That Never Flew* (2013) and *Almost Then* (2021), is also an award-winning filmmaker who focuses on empowering female sporting narratives and celebrating women's voices on film.

Hugh McMillan hails from rural Galloway. He is a well published, anthologised and broadcast poet, writer and performer. His last collection *Haphazardly in the Starless Night* was published in 2021 and *Diverted to Split*, his latest, is due out in summer 2024. In 2021, he was appointed editor of the Scottish Poetry Library's anthology *Best Scottish Poems* and was also chosen to be a Saltire Society judge for Best Scottish Poetry Collection of the Year. His cult classic, *McMillan's Galloway*, was reprinted in paperback form in May 2023.

Julie McNeill is the poet-in-residence for St Mirren FC Charitable Foundation, the only female poet attached to a professional football club (as far as we are aware) in the UK, perhaps the world. She is the Makar of The Hampden Collection and author of two poetry pamphlets, *Ragged Rainbows* (2021) and *Something Small* (2023). Her latest book, *We Are Scottish Football*, was released earlier this year (2024). She is also the co-author of the award-winning *Mission Dyslexia* series for neurodivergent children.

David McVey lectures at New College Lanarkshire. He writes short stories, non-fiction and the odd poem. He supports home-town team Kirkintilloch Rob Roy, Inverness CT by marriage, and the Scotland National Teams by affliction.

Sam Milne is a 39-year-old mum of two, who loves playing football, and is also a Club Equity Officer at the Scottish FA, covering Tayside and Fife – one of the six regions across the country.

Andy Mitchell is a sports historian who runs the website scottishsporthistory.com and has published many books and articles. He is a former Head of Communications at the Scottish FA.

Shaun Moore was spoiled. Introduced to football by his uncle taking him to see the 70s mix of Lisbon Lions and Quality Street Kids. A bookworm who played street football as everybody did then, but was rubbish at it, so remained a fan. And admirer of the poetic genius of some chants.

Tom Murray is based in Dumfries. He was a Scottish Poetry Library Poetry Ambassador 2021–23. His publications include *The Future is Behind You* (poetry), *Sins of the Father* (play), *The Clash* (play), *Out of My Head* (fiction), *There is a Place I Go* (poetry) and *The Permanent Room* (fiction).

Abiy Orr is proud to be an Aberdeenshire teuchter, having traced back seven generations of farming and fisherfolk. Beavering away in hope of that elusive writing break, she's always happy to tell her work colleagues exactly where to stick their semicolons!

Ann Park has enjoyed successful careers in technology and football. She is committed to addressing gender imbalance in both fields and, as Director of Community & Partnerships at Hearts FC, harnesses the power of football to build stronger communities.

Born in 1966, lifelong Killie fan, **Stuart Paterson**, author of several poetry collections in English and Scots and the first and so far only BBC Scotland poet-in-residence, lives in Nithsdale. His new book, *Stravaigs*, does what it'll say on the cover.

Jane Patience lives in East Dunbartonshire and studied creative writing at Glasgow University. Her short stories and poetry have been published in various anthologies and magazines, and have been broadcast on radio. Her family members are the inspiration for much of her poetry. She has many vices and does not apologise for any of them.

Aylei Pickup was born on the 9th of November 2009. A happy little girl with a cheeky smile and curly hair. She grew up with a love for dance and football. She did dance and gymnastics competitions then realised her passion was playing football. She played for the girls and the boys and is now playing for Spartans U16 (NPL level). She is now in high school thriving and studying for her exams.

Eddi Reader is regarded as one of Scotland's best singer-songwriters. She grew up in Glasgow and Irvine, and it was in those towns that she learned to use music as a vehicle for communicating with others through performing. She has been awarded three Brit Awards and an MBE. She is the proud granddaughter of, the equally legendary, Sadie Smith of Rutherglen Ladies FC.

Fiona Skillen is a Professor of History in the Department of Social Sciences, in the School for Business and Society at Glasgow Caledonian University. Her research focuses on women's sport during the late nineteenth and twentieth centuries, she has published extensively in this subject area. She regularly contributes to radio and television programmes on the history of sport. She has recently completed a FIFA-sponsored project on the history of women's football in Scotland, 1850–1939.

Gayle Smith is a spoken word poet from Baillieston who co-hosts Words And Music with her friend Jen Hughes. She is a transwoman and has been published in various anthologies and online publications. She is also a member of Women With Fierce Words poetry collective.

Gerda Stevenson is an award-winning writer, actor, director and singer-songwriter. Her work includes short story collection *Letting Go* (2021), poetry collections *Tomorrow's Feast* (2023), *Quines: Poems in Tribute to Women of Scotland* (2020) and *If This Were Real* (2013) – the latter two also published in Italian translations – and stage play 'Federer Versus Murray'. www.gerdastevenson.co.uk.

Bruce Strachan is a director, producer and lecturer in acting at Queen Margaret University. He has worked for Hull Truck, TAG, The Arches, The National Youth Theatre of Great Britain and the National Theatre of Scotland.

Cricketer, author, historian **Richard S Young** is busy penning his follow up to the groundbreaking *As the Willow Vanishes: Glasgow's Foreign Legacy* (2014), which will be released later this year. A founder and director of The Football's Square Mile he has been instrumental in telling the world the stories of cricket and football. And there's many more to come!

Stephen Watt is the Poetry Editor for *Nutmeg* football magazine, and is the former poet-in-residence for Dumbarton FC. His sixth poetry collection is due out later in 2024 and he has also been the editor of two punk poetry collections for the Joe Strummer Foundation and Buzzcocks.

TIPPERMUIR BOOKS

Tippermuir Books Ltd is an independent
publishing company based in Perth, Scotland.

PUBLISHING HISTORY

Spanish Thermopylae (2009)

Battleground Perthshire (2009)

Perth: Street by Street (2012)

Born in Perthshire (2012)

In Spain with Orwell (2013)

Trust (2014)

Perth: As Others Saw Us (2014)

Love All (2015)

A Chocolate Soldier (2016)

The Early Photographers of Perthshire (2016)

*Taking Detective Novels Seriously:
The Collected Crime Reviews of Dorothy L Sayers* (2017)

Walking with Ghosts (2017)

No Fair City: Dark Tales from Perth's Past (2017)

*The Tale o the Wee Mowdie that wantit tae ken wha
keeched on his heid* (2017)

*Hunters: Wee Stories from the Crescent:
A Reminiscence of Perth's Hunter Crescent* (2017)

A Little Book of Carol's (2018)

Flipstones (2018)

Perth: Scott's Fair City: The Fair Maid of Perth & Sir Walter Scott – A Celebration & Guided Tour (2018)

God, Hitler, and Lord Peter Wimsey: Selected Essays, Speeches and Articles by Dorothy L Sayers (2019)

Perth & Kinross: A Pocket Miscellany: A Companion for Visitors and Residents (2019)

The Piper of Tobruk: Pipe Major Robert Roy, MBE, DCM (2019)

The 'Gig Docter o Athole': Dr William Irvine & The Irvine Memorial Hospital (2019)

Afore the Highlands: The Jacobites in Perth, 1715–16 (2019)

'Where Sky and Summit Meet': Flight Over Perthshire – A History: Tales of Pilots, Airfields, Aeronautical Feats, & War (2019)

Diverted Traffic (2020)

Authentic Democracy: An Ethical Justification of Anarchism (2020)

'If Rivers Could Sing': A Scottish River Wildlife Journey. A Year in the Life of the River Devon as it flows through the Counties of Perthshire, Kinross-shire & Clackmannanshire (2020)

A Squatter o Bairnrhymes (2020)

In a Sma Room Songbook: From the Poems by William Soutar (2020)

The Nicht Afore Christmas: the much-loved yuletide tale in Scots (2020)

Ice Cold Blood (2021)

The Perth Riverside Nursery & Beyond: A Spirit of Enterprise and Improvement (2021)

Fatal Duty: Police Killers and Killer Cops:
the Scottish Police Force 1812–1952 (2021)

The Shanter Legacy: The Search for the Grey Mare's Tail (2021)

'Dying to Live': The Story of Grant McIntyre,
Covid's Sickest Patient (2021)

The Black Watch and the Great War (2021)

Beyond the Swelkie: A Collection of Poems & Writings to
Mark the Centenary of George Mackay Brown (2021)

Sweet F.A. (2022)

A War of Two Halves (2022)

A Scottish Wildlife Odyssey (2022)

In the Shadow of Piper Alpha (2022)

Mind the Links: Golf Memories (2022)

Perthshire 101: A Poetic Gazetteer of the Big County (2022)

The Banes o the Turas: An Owersettin in Scots o the Poems bi
Pino Mereu scrievit in Tribute tae Hamish Henderson (2022)

Walking the Antonine Wall: A Journey from East to West Scotland
(2022)

The Japan Lights: On the Trail of the Scot Who Lit Up Japan's Coast
(2022)

Fat Girl Best Friend: 'Claiming Our Space' –
Plus Size Women in Film & Television (2023)

Wild Quest Britain: A Nature Journey of Discovery through
England, Scotland & Wales – from Lizard Point to Dunnet Head
(2023)

Guid Mornin! Guid Nicht! (2023)

Madainn Mhath! Oidhche Mhath! (2023)

Who's Aldo? (2023)

A History of Irish Republicanism in Dundee (c1840 to 1985)
(Rùt Nic Foirbeis, 2024)

The Stone of Destiny & The Scots (John Hulbert, 2024)

*The Mysterious Case of the Stone of Destiny: A Scottish Historical
Detective Whodunnit!* (David Maule, 2024)

Salvage (Mark Baillie, 2024)

FORTHCOMING

*William Soutar: Collected Works, Volume 1 Published Poetry (1923–
1946)* (Paul S Philippou (Editor-in-Chief) & Kirsteen McCue
and Philippa Osmond-Williams (editors), 2024)

*William Soutar: Collected Works, Volume 2 Published Poetry (1948–
2000)* (Paul S Philippou (Editor-in-Chief) & Kirsteen McCue
and Philippa Osmond-Williams (editors), 2024)

*William Soutar: Collected Works, Volume 3 (Miscellaneous &
Unpublished Poetry)* (Paul S Philippou (Editor-in-Chief) &
Kirsteen McCue and Philippa Osmond-Williams (editors),
2026)

William Soutar: Collected Works, Volumes 4–6 (Prose Selections)
(Paul S Philippou (Editor-in-Chief) & Kirsteen McCue and
Philippa Osmond-Williams (editors), 2027+)

The Black Watch From the Crimean War to the Egyptian Campaign
(Derek Patrick and Fraser Brown (editors), 2024)

Drystone: A Gathering of Terminology and Technique
(Nick Aitken, 2024)

The Scottish Murder Book: Sensational Scottish Murder Trials. Book 1: Perth, Angus and Fife (Mark Bridgeman, 2024)

Perthshire's Pound of Flesh (Mark Bridgeman, 2024)

The Lass and the Quine (Ashley Douglas (writer), Katie Osmond (illustrator), 2025)

The Royal Edinburgh Military Tattoo: 'The Show Must Go On' – Travels of the Tattoo Producer
(Brigadier Sir Melville Jameson, 2024)

Balkan Rhapsody (Maria Kassimova-Moisset, translated from the Bulgarian by Iliyana Nedkova, edited by Cara Blacklock, 2024)

Button Bog And Other Voices & Treasures From A Traveller's Kist (Jess Smith, 2024)

A Wildlife Guide to Edinburgh (Keith Broomfield, 2024/5)

The Road to Mons Graupius (Alan Montgomery, 2024/5)

The Whole Damn Town (Hannah Ballantyne, 2025)